Goalkeeping for soccer

Techniques, Skills and Practices

Simon Smith

Foreword by
Sir Bobby Robson

ISBN-13: 978-1-902523-66-0
ISBN-10: 1-902523-66-0

Author: Simon Smith
Editor: Sharon Cawood
Designer: Leanne Taylor

First Edition
Editor: Chris Rigg
Typesetter: Catherine Worsley
Illustrator: Jo Willard

Photographs courtesy of actionplus sports images, adidas, Simon Smith, Lee Fraser and Ian Horricks.
The author would also like to thank Sue Miller for her contribution.

The author recognises that goalkeepers may be male or female.
However, for simplicity, the goalkeepers in this book are referred to as male.

Published by
Coachwise Business Solutions
Chelsea Close
Off Amberley Road
Armley
Leeds LS12 4HP

Tel: 0113-231 1310 Fax: 0113-231 9606

Email: enquiries@coachwise.ltd.uk Website: www.1st4sport.com

050445

As a football manager, working with the players I've had in front of me day in, day out and honing the players of the future has been my life, and I'm proud of the achievements and successes of the teams and clubs with which I've been associated over the years.

When I arrived at Newcastle United in 1999, Simon Smith was responsible for overseeing the progress of the club's goalkeepers. It is a privilege for me to endorse his goalkeeping coaching manual. This book draws on his years of goalkeeping experience, both as a professional player and as a top-flight coach. He knows first-hand exactly what it feels like to be between the posts. That in itself is so important. You can't beat a 'soldier being on the battlefield'. Through his coaching of the club's senior goalkeepers and his work with youngsters starting out in the game, he has amply demonstrated he has the expertise to get the very best out of players at all levels.

Compared with outfield players, goalkeepers have been neglected when it comes to textbooks that help footballers understand their craft, and yet no great team is complete without them. The techniques, practices, strategies and tactics that Simon has set out here will massively enrich the knowledge and skills of these players and their coaches. It will add to their knowledge at all levels, whether they are starting out as a coach or player or have years of experience behind them.

Readers of this book will not need me to tell them that goalkeepers are key players in a team. They need techniques, skills, good handling, bravery, decision making and consistency, all of which come through the sort of 'perfect practice' that Simon talks about. Goalkeepers also need to be able to work and communicate with the rest of the defence, so they have an understanding between them that is 'sixth sense'.

But the very best goalkeepers I have worked with have also had some significant extras: dedication, passion, top-level fitness and agility, along with the courage to be the last man between the ball and the back of the net. Goalkeepers should never forget that they can play a monumental part in a team, save a game and make a championship. I am certain that this book will help them do just that.

Bobby Robson

Foreword to First Edition

At last a serious goalkeeping coaching book for both goalkeepers and coaches who want to improve their skills, written by someone who has dedicated his life to the number one position – Simon Smith.

I first met Simon when I was doing a coaching demonstration at Lilleshall for The Football Association. It was obvious from the outset that here was a man who was doing everything in his power to become as knowledgeable as he could about goalkeeping.

Since that first meeting we have become firm friends and I have had the opportunity to watch Simon grow and develop into the excellent goalkeeping coach he is today. When I became manager at Carlisle United and no longer had time to look after the goalkeepers myself, I immediately rang Simon to ask him to come and take over their coaching.

They have all benefited from his studious approach to the position and now it is your turn; this book gives you the insight into the techniques, skills and practices that are required to improve, either as a goalkeeper or as a coach. As a serious student of goalkeeping, I am sure that this book will become a very important tool in your search for perfection.

Mervyn Day (First Team Coach, Charlton Athletic)

Contents

Contents

THE SPECIALIST

The goalkeeper is a specialist player but nevertheless an integral part of a football team, with considerable influence and responsibility within the team. Having a goalkeeper who is reliable and consistent is important to any team which wants to be successful. The goalkeeper, more than any other player, can win or lose games single handed – that is why goalkeepers are different. They are a breed apart, not only because they are the only team members who can use their hands but also because of the responsibility placed on their shoulders. The goalkeeper is the linchpin of the defence and can play a major part in initiating attacks from the defensive third. As the last line of defence, the saves and errors of a goalkeeper are more prominent than those of other players.

Goalkeeping is a specialist position; it therefore requires specialist coaching and as much practice as is physically possible. The purpose of this book is to outline the basic techniques and suggest ways to set practices and deliver those techniques. *Practice does not make perfect, practice makes permanent, perfect practice makes perfect*[1]. This book will give goalkeepers and coaches an insight into the goalkeeper's make-up and the challenges he may face.

In my experience, aspiring young goalkeepers take a special interest in their position, talking about specialised kit and watching top goalkeepers in action, perhaps recognising the fact that goalkeepers at all levels face similar types of situations and problems. Playing other sports which require and encourage catching and movement (eg rugby, basketball, volleyball) should be encouraged. Pat Jennings, the former Spurs, Arsenal and Northern Ireland goalkeeper, put much of his early development down to playing Gaelic football at school; this helped him with his handling, kicking and the ability to withstand physical challenges. Jennings is remembered for his ability to catch the ball with one hand and his skill in kicking the ball great distances, both of which are throw-backs to his early Gaelic football experiences. Bruce Grobbelaar, the Liverpool and Zimbabwe goalkeeper, was a multi-talented games player in his development years; he played basketball, cricket and baseball – all of which helped him with movement and coordination.

Jean-Paul Sartre, the French philosopher, suggested that the tactical role of the goalkeeper within the game is to be in a position, at several points during a game, to save his side. This would involve going beyond his capability in an individual act.

Bruce Grobbelaar's philosophy on goalkeeping expresses one of the aims of this goalkeeping book: *The aim is to catch the ball whenever possible ... I know I am guilty of dropping a few but I do catch more than I drop ... enjoy your sport, when it stops being fun, stop playing*. The goalkeeper who prevents the ball going into the goal most frequently is the better goalkeeper; how he does this is of secondary importance. Many coaches will have come across a goalkeeper who has great technique in closed practice but somehow seems to let the ball in the goal during games.

ATTRIBUTES

The top class goalkeeper has many attributes, both physical and psychological. These include:

*   self-confidence
*   good attitude
*   technical ability
*   mental strength
*   physical strength
*   opportunity
*   luck.

1   Kiostis, P. *Golf Digest*, June 1992.

Goalkeeping is a combination of many factors, both physical and mental. Many people have developed the idea that you have to be mad to be a goalkeeper. This comes from the courage needed to throw yourself under the feet of on-rushing forwards, as well as the ability to handle the mental pressure of making a mistake, both of which are part and parcel of the game. Goalkeepers who make the fewest mistakes and handle them well are often regarded as the best.

Psychological attributes include the following:

- fearless and brave
- committed and dedicated
- able to concentrate and remain focused for long periods
- willing to train hard
- a desire to keep the ball out of the goal
- able to make decisions and act on them.

Goalkeepers should work to improve the following areas of their mental game, as these will considerably enhance their performance on the field:

- Match **concentration** enables the goalkeeper's agility to be used at precisely the right time. Ninety minutes of full concentration ensures the goalkeeper is aware of what is happening in front of him at all times.
- **Courage** and determination are essential qualities of a goalkeeper.
- Good **anticipation** is very important to goalkeepers. The ability to see the danger of attack a fraction of a second before it actually happens allows the goalkeeper to call defenders to cut out the danger or move into a position which makes the saves easier.
- Peripheral **vision** helps the goalkeeper to see how the opposition are lining up.
- Good **communication** is essential to the goalkeeper. Calling defenders into positions to cut out the danger will reduce the possibility of a shot or cross towards goal.

Physical attributes include the following:

- speed, agility, balance
- fast reflexes
- good coordination
- height.

Goalkeepers come in all shapes and sizes and there are no set rules about height, reach, speed or shape. It appears that managers and coaches alike are looking for goalkeepers who look *big* in front of the net and have a physical presence (a fact seen by looking at the average height of Premier League goalkeepers). This gives defenders confidence, forwards a smaller target and the goalkeeper the ability to resist the physical challenges which are part and parcel of the game. As a coach you will have to take each of these factors into consideration. Goalkeepers require anaerobic power rather than aerobic endurance[1]; this fact determines the type of training needed by the goalkeeper and also sets him apart from outfield players who require greater levels of aerobic endurance.

---

1   Anaerobic power is used for activities of short duration and high intensity. Aerobic endurance is used for activities of long duration and low intensity.

Height is obviously a great advantage when dealing with high balls in the penalty area; it may also give added reach. Anywhere between 185–190cm (6'0"–6'2") is ideal. Having said that, the smaller goalkeepers may be particularly agile and have great spring, and those who are particularly tall need to have great agility to collapse quickly to the ground for low shots. One problem with taller goalkeepers is that due to their height advantage, they do not always attack the ball as they should. The **reach** of the goalkeeper will influence whether or not he can catch a ball; a goalkeeper with lesser reach may only be able to parry or deflect the ball. **Speed** is an essential quality of the goalkeeper. Speed of movement, but not necessarily running, is of great help as goalkeeping is all about movement; moving into the line of the ball and down the line of the ball. Good **agility** (the ability to move quickly and fluently) and **flexibility** are also required.

Whatever physical size, the goalkeeper needs to be the captain of the penalty area; that is not to say that everything in that penalty area should be caught by the goalkeeper, but it is a goalkeeper's job to organise defenders within this area and to keep them at a distance, to enable him to have enough space in which to work.

SKILLS AND TECHNICAL ASPECTS

There is no magic formula to goalkeeping – it is based on sound technique and a certain amount of agility. At introductory level, there are two key areas to goalkeeping:

- the ability to catch the ball
- correct movement.

Although listed separately, they are very closely connected because without one you cannot do the other. Good goalkeepers are often described as being in the right place at the right time; in many cases this is due to good movement which is linked to anticipation. In most cases, upper body movement comes first, coupled with the correct footwork, moving the goalkeepers into a position to enable them to use the correct handling technique or having made one save, get up and move to a new position to make another save.

Being able to catch the ball cleanly means that the:

- goalkeeper's team retains possession
- goalkeepers can create possible scoring opportunities with quick, accurate distribution.

Goalkeeping is about catching the ball if at all possible – at whatever height, speed or distance in order to keep the ball out of the goal. Young goalkeepers should be encouraged to watch as many top goalkeepers as possible, as they will learn things that coaches may not be able to show them.

The goalkeeper's main concern is to reduce the chance of a goal being scored against him. The three main principles are:

- coaching and organising defenders to cut out danger before it reaches him
- being in the right starting position and distance from the ball
- getting to the ball as early as possible, whether it is from crosses or shots, allowing the goalkeeper to make fast interceptions.

As I have already pointed out, the basic elements of all techniques are footwork and handling; every goalkeeper must aim to perfect basic technique. At a higher level of goalkeeping, basic technique should not be practised in isolation; training sessions should incorporate a degree of *match situations* where the introduction of rebounds and second saves can be included.

Goalkeeping can be made easier by good communication with defenders. By giving clear information, the goalkeeper may enable defenders to deal with situations before the ball reaches a danger area where the goalkeeper is needed.

Rule changes

The rule change preventing the pass-back from being handled has meant that goalkeepers have had to become competent outfield players; they need the first touch of the centre forward, the range of passing and vision of a midfield player and the heading and tackling ability of a defender. The automatic red card for illegal challenges either inside or outside the penalty area has meant that goalkeepers have had to adopt a more cautious approach; their judgement and timing need to be precise and this has highlighted the need to practise the one vs one situation.

COACHING AND EQUIPMENT

Like many other methods of coaching, my method is based on match analysis and practices relating to complex match situations – in other words, basic techniques are not practised in isolation but combined with other activities (ie distribution in order to make the practice situation more like a match situation). As goalkeepers become more competent at the basic techniques, they can build up their own game with the help of the coach who provides realistic, simple practices.

Mental preparation is a positive, mental approach to keeping the ball out of the net. The coach should encourage the goalkeeper to remove any negative thoughts from his mind prior to training and matches. Focusing must be encouraged during shooting practices (ie each player has ten shots, the goalkeeper works at 75% max for the first six then works at 100% for the final four). This simple habit enables the goalkeeper to practise focusing and concentrating on the prime role, to stop the ball at all costs, rather than just getting in the habit of standing in goal.

Self-evaluation

Goalkeepers should always be encouraged to identify their own faults, even if they need to be prompted. If they can see their own weaknesses, they may work harder at correcting them, as opposed to having to trust the word of what they may view as a critical coach. Asking a goalkeeper what to work on can be a good idea but the coach must ensure that every attempt is made to rectify technical deficiencies. Coaching should be a two-way process rather than a dictatorial one.

Equipment

Goalkeeping gloves have dramatically changed the techniques goalkeepers need to use. In days gone by, especially on wet days, the only way to gather the ball was into the body. The introduction of goalkeeping gloves, with the excellent grip they offer, has meant it is possible for goalkeepers to get a secure grip on the ball without taking it into the body. This can have a negative effect – goalkeepers become lazy and sloppy with their techniques. It is therefore vital that the coach reinforces the importance of getting two surfaces behind the ball at all times and also that it is the hands inside the gloves which do the catching, not the gloves. Some coaches believe that youngsters should practise the basic handling techniques without gloves. While this is a good idea, the gloves can give youngsters extra confidence when learning to catch the ball.

One final note, goalkeepers are the most important players on the pitch – they are the first line of attack and the last line of defence. Logically, the goalkeeper should receive quality and continuous coaching in order to give the team the best possible chance of winning. All aspects of goalkeeping should be performed accurately and confidently; training should be aimed at flexibility, linked with agility and at all times good technique.

Successful goalkeeping is based on sound technique. In this section we look at the techniques and how they should be used. Like other techniques, there are simple guidelines to follow; having the ability to catch the ball is a basic necessity for all goalkeepers. To achieve this, the goalkeeper should start in the correct position to receive the ball.

Pane of Glass Theory

Imagine that you have a pane of glass in front of you, six inches in front of your feet. You must catch or make contact with the oncoming ball before it hits or smashes the glass. How?

Head: forward, with eyes firmly fixed on the ball

Hands: in front of feet, shoulder-width apart, elbows in front of the line of the body, fingers pointing towards the ball

Feet: with weight on the front studs.

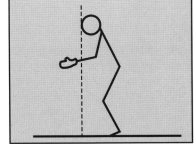

Figure 1

Leading with the hands

By starting with the hands forward, it enables you to lead with your hands as the ball approaches, which has three advantages:

1   it enables you to 'watch' the ball into your hands

2   it lets you follow any movement of the ball coming towards you with your hands

3   it enables you to take the pace off the ball, using your arms as 'shock absorbers', while keeping the ball forward so that you can still see the ball and keep your elbows tucked in.

Figure 2

Diving

Head: behind the ball

Hands: leading with your hands, take the ball as early as possible and keep your elbows in front of the line of the body

Feet: step off the nearest foot to the ball, off the front studs, foot at 45°.

If you are unable to catch the ball and therefore need to parry it – by adopting the above position – it enables you to push the ball to safety as opposed to letting the ball push your hand back.

Figure 3

THE STARTING POSITION

The goalkeeper's starting position on the pitch depends on the specific situation. You should consider the:

- position of the ball in relation to the goal
- quality of the forward
- quality of the goalkeeper.

Starting position one: the recognised starting position

The starting position and movement of a goalkeeper can be compared with a tennis player receiving a serve. Goalkeepers set themselves in a receiving position, then make a small jump, widening their stance; this movement tenses the muscles allowing goalkeepers to move quickly.

Main coaching points

- Feet are shoulder-width apart (Figure 4).
- Knees are slightly bent (Figure 4).
- The head is tilted forward and steady, bringing the weight onto the balls of the feet (Figure 4).
- Elbows are tucked into the waist with the hands at waist height, shoulder-width apart and pointing towards the ball with the fingers outstretched (Figure 4).
- As the attacker begins to shoot, the stance is widened.
- The hands move into a receiving position as the ball approaches.
- For balls above the waist, the thumbs come together, fingers spread behind the ball, with the elbows tucked in, giving a tighter grip on the ball (Figure 5).
- For balls below the waist, the hands lower, the little fingers come together and the fingers spread. The hands remain in front of the body with the elbows tucked in (Figure 6).

Figure 4

Figure 5

Figure 6

Starting position two: the starting position to run

This is used in general play and allows the goalkeeper to move forward and backward.

Main coaching points

- One foot is placed in front of the other.
- The body and hand positions are the same as Starting Position One (Figure 7).

Figure 7

Starting position three: the low crouch position

This is used in one versus one situations and when the goalkeeper is close to the ball.

Main coaching points

- The goalkeeper is balanced, relaxed and ready to move in any direction.
- The body and hand positions are the same as Starting position one (Figure 8).

Figure 8

In all three positions, the hands should remain in front of the line of the body for the following reasons:

- It enables the goalkeeper to watch the ball all the way into his hands, while remaining balanced.
- It creates a distance between the hands and the body, enabling the arms to act as shock absorbers.
- The gap between the hands and body means there is less likelihood of the ball rebounding off the body.
- The gap also allows the goalkeeper to recover the ball if it is dropped when making the initial catch, before it goes behind the line of his body.
- If making a diving save, taking the ball in front of the line of the body encourages the goalkeeper to come across and forward, keeping the all-important bottom elbow from becoming trapped under the body (this is explained in more detail in Section Three).

BALANCE AND FOOTWORK

When moving, goalkeepers must maintain good balance with their weight distributed on the balls of their feet, the head forward and the hands in a catching position. At all times they should be relaxed and comfortable.

The goalkeeper's balance needs to be like a boxer's, with the body weight moving forward whenever possible. This is achieved by getting *the nose in front of the feet*.

Goalkeepers must always remain balanced when moving. If they are moving from the right, lead with the head and the rest of the body will then begin to follow. The right foot is then moved across the left foot in a stepping movement, followed by moving the left foot across in a sideways shuffle or gliding movement until the goalkeeper is in line with the approaching ball; this is done without the two feet coming in contact. The same applies with step and dive movements. Goalkeepers take off from the leg nearer to the ball. If they take off from the leg further from the ball, the distance covered will not be as great.

There are three types of movement commonly used by goalkeepers: the sideways skip, the cross-legged run and running.

The sideways skip

- In this movement, the feet travel just above the turf in a sideways motion, without touching.

- It is critical that the feet do not cross, as this would affect the balance which is needed to keep the head steady.

- Throughout the movement, the hands should be in a catching position (Figure 9).

Figure 9

The cross-legged run

- This is used for moving quickly across the goal to intercept a ball or to change position for a cross.

- It is a faster method of movement than sideways skipping.

- This method maintains an open body position with the chest facing the ball and will allow a sideways dive (Figure 10).

Figure 10

Running

- Running and sprinting are only to be used as a last resort if the goalkeeper is in trouble. However, there will always be times when it is needed in a game situation.

MOVING INTO AND DOWN THE LINE

Moving into the line

This refers to moving into the line of flight of the ball so that if a triangle was drawn between the two posts and the attacker, the goalkeeper would be positioned on the centre line of the triangle (see Figure 11). This only applies if the attacker is coming straight at the goal; if the ball is in a wider position, goalkeepers must protect their near post, which is the more vulnerable. This will give goalkeepers a narrow, near post area to cover and a wider, far post area. Goalkeepers should be positioned so they can cover the narrow area in one step and the wider area in a step and a dive. By doing this, they should be able to intercept all shots at goal, even on the wider side, as the ball has to cover a greater distance and therefore takes more time.

Moving into the line of flight of the ball should be relatively simple. Goalkeepers should lead with their head and then their hands, and the rest of their body should follow.

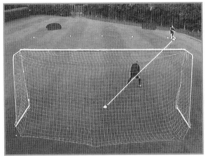

Figure 11

Moving down the line

Having moved into the line of the ball, goalkeepers must now move down the line. This will have the effect of reducing the target for the attacker (see Figure 12). If goalkeepers do not move far enough down the line of the ball, they will not be able to cover all the goal (see Figure 13); however, if they move too far, they will be susceptible to a chip shot. Goalkeepers must only move down the line when the attacker's head is down, looking at the ball, or if he is out of shooting distance. Once the attacker is close enough to shoot and looks up to prepare himself, the goalkeeper must set himself in the receiving position. Even if the goalkeeper is out of position, he can set himself to make a save but if he is still moving forward, it is very difficult to dive sideways.

Moving into the line and down the line is often referred to as *narrowing the angle*. Each time the angle of the ball changes, the goalkeeper must adjust his position to achieve the correct relationship to the ball. To move effectively, the goalkeeper must use the correct footwork.

Figure 12

Figure 13

STOPPING THE BALL

Having taken up the correct starting position and moved into the line of flight of the ball, the goalkeeper must decide which technique of stopping the ball is appropriate. The technique used will depend on the height and speed of the approaching ball.

Taking balls at ground level

There are two different techniques: the stoop and sidefoot control. Coaching points are provided for each technique.

The stoop

- Move into the line of the ball, bringing the feet together to form a secondary barrier.

- Bend from the hips.

- Bring the little fingers together, open the palms and point the fingers towards the ground.

- The ball must be taken as early as possible and then cupped into the chest (Figure 14).

Figure 14

Sidefoot control

With the introduction of the laws regarding the pass-back, goalkeepers are now having to use their feet to control the ball:

- Move into the line of the ball.

- Use the side of the foot to stop the ball in front of the line of the body.

- If the ball is in front, it gives a better angle to clear the ball (Figure 15).

Figure 15

Taking balls at waist height

Main coaching points

- Keep the palms open and the little fingers together.

- Allow the ball into the waist and cup hands around the back of the ball with weight remaining forward (Figure 16).

Figure 16

Taking balls at chest height

There are two different techniques: into the chest and above the chest. Coaching points are provided for each technique.

In front of the chest

- A ball which is travelling at pace and on a flat trajectory can be caught in front of the line of the body.

- The elbows are tucked in with the arms nearly straight.

- The thumbs are touching and the fingers spread.

- The head must be steady with the eyes fixed on the ball.

- The ball is caught as early as possible so it can be watched into the hands and the arms used as shock absorbers.

- Once the ball is caught, it should be held in that position to allow the goalkeeper the option to distribute the ball as early as possible (Figure 17).

Figure 17

Into the chest

- If the ball is between waist and chest height, it should be cupped into the chest, relaxing the chest on impact.

- There are other instances when this technique should be used. If the goalkeeper is young and his hands are not big enough to span the ball, catching it in front of the chest without palming it down is very difficult. It should also be used when the ball is coming very fast and safety is the main concern (Figure 18).

Figure 18

Taking the ball at head height

Main coaching points

- Move into the line of the ball.

- The hands move upwards with the thumbs touching and the fingers spread.

- The arms reach towards the ball, taking it as early as possible in front of the head. This enables the goalkeeper to watch the ball all the way into the hands.

- The arms must be bent to allow some shock absorption to take place (Figure 19).

- The hands should be placed behind and to the side of the ball (Figure 20).

- The ball should be brought into the chest unless an early release is possible.

- The head should be used as a secondary barrier and kept steady at all times.

Figure 19

Figure 20

Taking the ball above head height

Main coaching points

- The technique is the same as for balls at head height, except that the arms are nearly straight as they reach to catch the ball in front of the head.

- The head is tilted back to watch the ball into the hands, with the eyes firmly fixed on the ball (Figure 21).

Figure 21

Practices

Key

| GK | = | Goalkeeper | X | = | Cone | = ● | Ball |

GK = Goalkeeper   X = Cone   = ● Ball

S = Server   **A** = Attacker   = Penalty spot

→ = Movement of person ----▶ = Movement of ball ◄—▶ = Distance

NB When running the practices, always use the coaching points in the preceding section.

Practice 1

The ball is served at various heights, from both the foot and the hand.

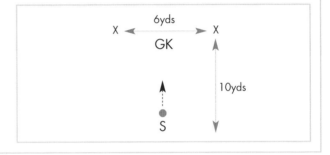

Practice 2

As Practice 1 but the server plays the ball to the side of the goalkeeper.

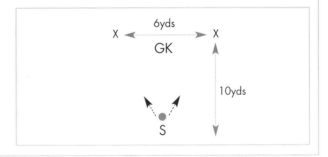

Practice 3

As Practice 1 but with two servers.

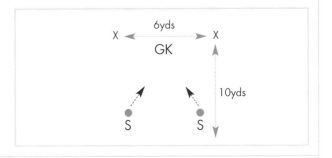

Practice 4

In pairs, one ball between two; one in the goal and the other with the ball on the marker. Goalkeeper 1A with the ball serves the ball to his partner 2A who saves it. The service can be a volley, half volley or from the floor. After goalkeeper 2A has made his save, he jogs to swop places with his partner. After both goalkeepers have saved, they move on to the next marker and the other pair (1B/2B) take their turn on the previous marker.

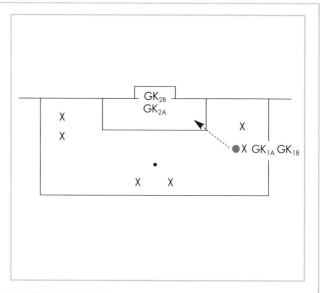

Practice 5

The server volleys the ball while the goalkeeper is moving forward. The goalkeeper must stop and adopt the starting position in order to make the save.

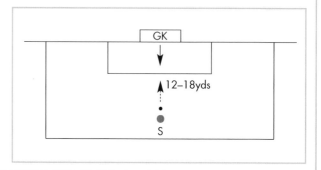

Practice 6

Server 1 serves high, server 2 serves at waist height and server 3 serves low. The goalkeeper must move along the line, dealing with each ball using the correct footwork.

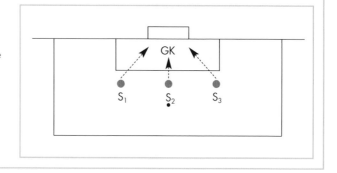

Practice 7

The server dribbles up to the cone and moves inside or outside of it, then shoots. The goalkeeper must adjust his position as necessary.

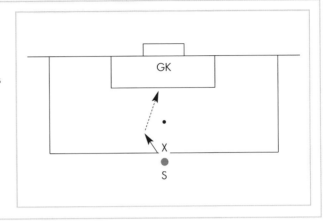

Practice 8

Goalkeeper 1B assumes a leap frog position; goalkeeper 1A jumps over 1B; as he lands, he adopts his starting position; as he does so, the server volleys the ball – after making the save, the goalkeeper must move backwards using the correct footwork (6-8 reps).

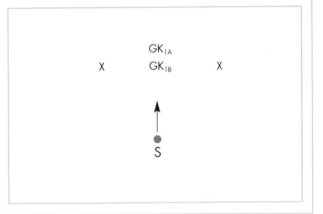

Practice 9

As above, but goalkeeper 1A goes through the legs of goalkeeper 1B, then makes his save. 1A progression is for goalkeeper 1A – as he has come either over or under – to either save the ball or leave it, so goalkeeper 1B must then react and make a save.

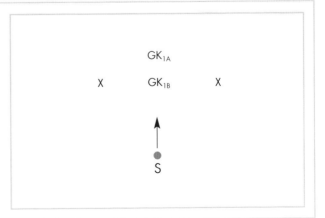

Moving into the line and down the line

Practice 1

Server 1 starts with the ball; he can either shoot or play the ball left to server 2 or right to server 3. The goalkeeper must move into the line and if possible down the line to make the goal look smaller. As the server is about to strike the ball, make sure the goalkeeper adopts the starting position and is still.

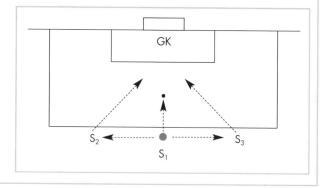

Practice 2

The goalkeeper stands at the post, sideways on and facing away from the goal. On command, the goalkeeper turns, moving into the small goal positioned on the six-yard line, trying to move into and down the line. As the goalkeeper approaches the small goal, the server can shoot. Use both sides.

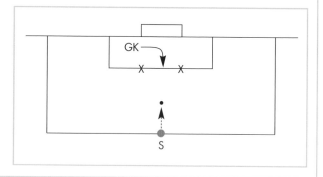

Practice 3

The goalkeeper is in a triangle facing the server, who volleys the ball at the goalkeeper who catches, throws the ball back to the server, and then moves his feet to face server 2 (10 reps).

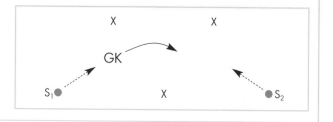

Practice 4

As above but with the goalkeeper facing each server, the goalkeeper makes a catch and then they change places (10 reps).

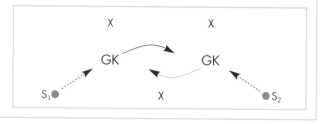

Practice 5

The goalkeeper jogs forward and touches the marker, after touching the marker the server can shoot at any time, then moves back towards the goal, making sure the goalkeeper is set as the server strikes.

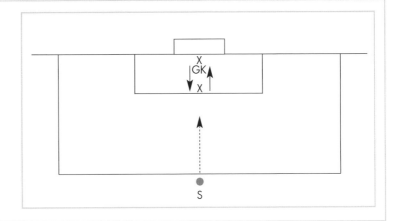

Practice 6

The goalkeeper facing into play spins off the marker into the small goal setting, getting into line as quickly as possible.

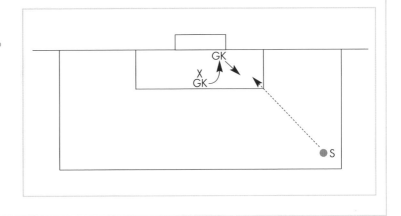

Practice 7

The server moves from the marker into post and then into the small goal setting, getting into line as quickly as possible.

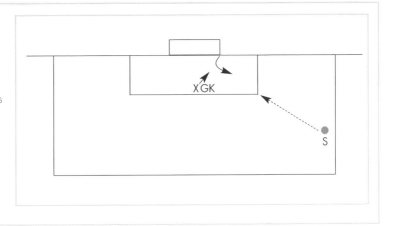

Practice 8

As the goalkeeper jogs forward, the goalkeeper is given command 1, 2, 3. The goalkeeper must get into that small goal as quickly as possible and be 'set' as the server shoots.

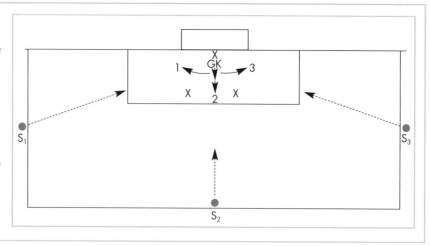

Practice 9

Server 1 plays a diagonal ball into A1 who controls the ball and shoots. Repeat with Server 2 and A2. The goalkeeper must move into line and down the line in order to make the save.

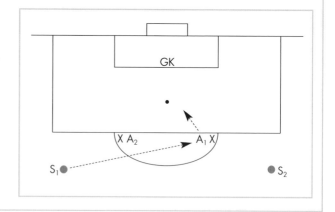

Practice 10

The goalkeeper serves the ball to the attacking Y's who come out as a pair to attack – the defending Z players come out to defend from a forward marker as the ball is thrown creating a two v two.

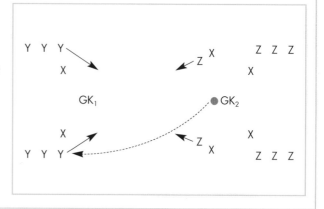

Footwork drills

Practice 1

Move over the balls by running, double-footed jumping (over each ball) and double-footed jumping (two balls forward, one back). On completion, run to the back of the queue.

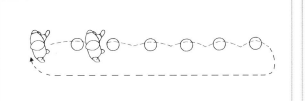

Practice 2

Move in and out of the balls sideways, backwards and forwards. On completion, run to the back of the queue.

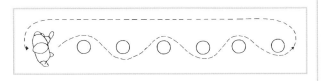

Practice 3

Weave in and out of the cones moving forwards, backwards and sideways.

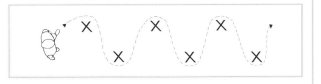

Practice 4

Move through the cones following the foot placements shown. After the start, one foot should land outside the cones and then both feet inside.

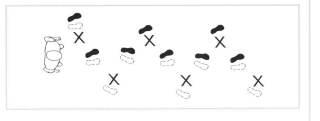

Practice 5

Alternately, servers 1 and 2 throw the ball overarm into the coned areas which are 1-metre wide from each post; the ball must bounce before it reaches the coned areas. The goalkeeper must move into a position to save.

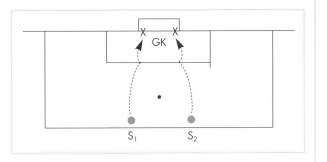

Practice 6

Servers 1 and 2 volley alternately to the side of the goalkeeper. The goalkeeper moves into the line of the ball to save (10–15 reps).

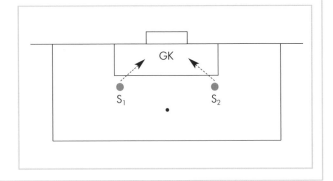

Practice 7

Goalkeeper 1 takes the lead and using the correct footwork, tries to beat his opponent to the marker of his choice. Goalkeeper 1 leads for five turns then goalkeeper 2 leads. The goalkeepers must return to the middle after each turn.

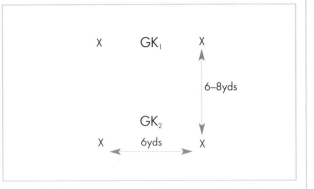

Practice 8

The goalkeeper stands in the goal facing server 1. Server 1 can volley, half-volley or strike the ball from the ground. The goalkeeper must make his save, return the ball to server 1, then turn quickly, moving forward through the goal to face server 2 (10 reps). Service may be changed to a throw above the goalkeeper's head, to work on footwork and take-off for catching crosses.

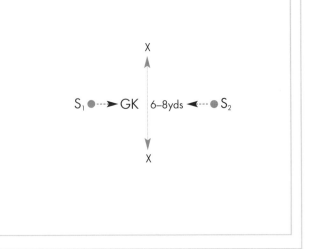

Practice 9

The goalkeeper is in the small goal facing server 1 who volleys the ball at the goalkeeper who makes a save and returns the ball to server 1; the goalkeeper then turns quickly and moves into the other small goal to face server 2 who serves the ball (8-10 reps); service may vary – volley or high throw.

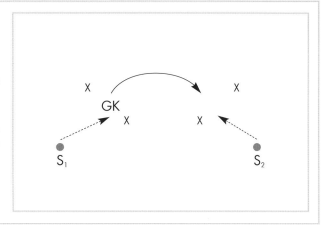

Practice 10

The goalkeeper starts side-on and moves through the cones – forward and back. As he comes forward between the two markers, the server facing volleys the ball at the goalkeeper's body, causing him to set himself in order to make the save before moving around the next markers.

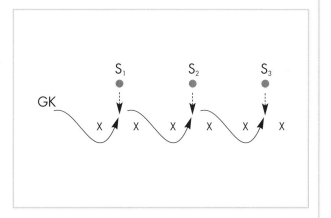

Practice 11

The goalkeeper starts in the middle of the goal; server 1 and server 2 stand 1 yard inside each post, approximately 8–10 yards out; using the correct footwork, the goalkeeper has to move to the goal to catch the ball; service must be timed and can be served by hand or foot, high or low.

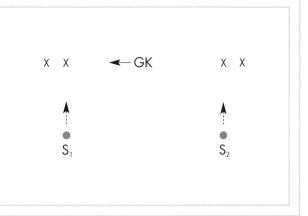

Having narrowed the angle and moved down the line, it may not be possible to stay in that position and make a save. Goalkeepers may have to make diving saves in order to stop the ball entering the goal.

Main coaching points

1 Take off from the leg nearer to the ball and turn the nearer foot out. This provides direction for the dive and uses the thigh muscle more efficiently.

2 Lead with the hands, trying to dive across and forward. Take the ball as early as possible with both hands together.

3 The goalkeeper should try to get his head behind the ball and as near as possible to it, as this gives extra momentum.

4 The goalkeeper should fall on his hip and shoulder and not his elbow, which can cause the ball to be jarred out of his hands (Figure 22).

5 Eyes should be firmly fixed on the ball.

6 The ball should be trapped on the ground, with one hand on top and one hand behind the ball and the goalkeeper's weight forwards. This allows the goalkeeper to recover quickly back onto his feet.

7 Keeping the body open allows a clear view of the ball. This lets the goalkeeper make slight adjustments, even with a deflected shot.

8 When it is not possible to hold the ball, it should be deflected with an open palm, keeping the wrist stiff and the eyes fixed on the ball.

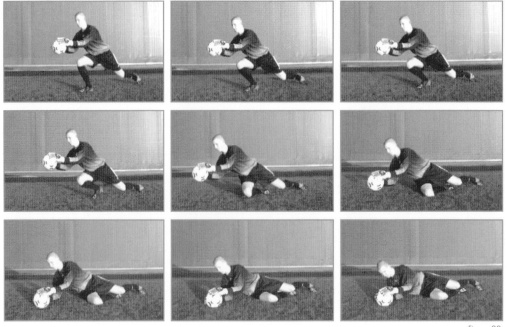

Figure 22

COLLAPSING SAVES

Ground shots to the side of the body are extremely difficult to save and require the goalkeeper to make a quick collapsing movement to get his body behind the ball ensuring his legs are flicked out from under him. A common fault in the rush to collapse is that goalkeepers forget to or cannot get their hands to the ball quickly enough. Occasionally when adjusting and narrowing the angle, goalkeepers will be too close to the attacker and will not have time to collapse to the ground. In this instance, goalkeepers will have to make saves with their feet or legs by blocking or pushing the ball away.

Main coaching points

• Prepare the hands early and place them in front of the body – this helps with the collapsing movement.

• As the ball reaches the hands, collapse the legs.

• Collect the ball into the chest.

Figure 23

ONE VERSUS ONE

When narrowing the angle, if an attacker is clear of the defence, the goalkeeper must make an instant decision – is it possible to win the race to the ball?

If the goalkeeper decides that he *can* win the race to the ball, he must move and collect the ball as early as possible; this decision will depend on the goalkeeper's starting position. If the goalkeeper does *not* think he can win the race to the ball, he must take the appropriate action to deal with an oncoming attacking player in possession of the ball. They are now in a one vs one situation.

There are three different stages to facing a one vs one situation:

Main coaching points

- The goalkeeper moves into and then down the line of the ball. This should be done as quickly as possible but the goalkeeper must still be able to stop and become balanced in a low crouch starting position. The goalkeeper stays on his feet and makes himself into as big a target as possible to reduce shooting opportunities and force the attacker into making a further move if he attempts to dribble around the goalkeeper (Figure 24).

- If the goalkeeper can move close enough to the attacker before he can shoot, he should be able to make a save. He should lead with his hands, making his body into a long barrier and diving when the ball is away from the attacker's feet (Figure 25).

- The ball should be caught with two hands and held firmly (Figure 26).

Figure 24

Figure 25

Figure 26

RECOVERY BACK TO GOAL

Goalkeepers are compelled to come off their line to cut down the shooting angle – as a result they can be caught out by a clever chipped shot or a high looping ball spinning up from a blocked challenge. Having to recover backwards to catch the ball or push the ball over the bar is extremely difficult.

Main coaching points

- Turn the body sideways-on and skip backwards to try to get under the ball.
- Take off from the nearer leg to the goal and using the arm nearer to the ball, with a stiff wrist and an open palm, push the ball over the bar.
- The head must remain steady throughout with the eyes on the ball at all times.
- Allow the momentum of the shot to take the ball over and beyond the bar (Figure 27).

Figure 27

Practices

Key

GK	=	Goalkeeper	X	=	Cone	= ●	Ball
S	=	Server	A	=	Attacker	=	Penalty spot
→	=	Movement of Person	---►	=	Movement of Ball	◄─► =	

Distance

NB When running the practices, always use the coaching points in the preceding section.

The key faults that should be looked for are:
- leading with the hand furthest from the ball
- moving the foot further from the ball first.

Practice 1

The goalkeeper stands a metre and a half to the side and in front of his partner who holds the ball in one outstretched hand. The goalkeeper dives across and takes the ball, in front of the line of his body, out of his partner's hand. He should fall on the side of his knee, hip and shoulder with the elbow nearer to the ground in front of his body.

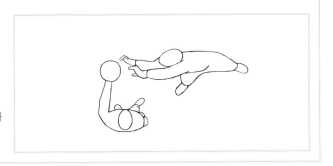

Practice 2

As Practice 1 but the service is a two-handed throw. The goalkeeper dives across to catch the ball. The principles of the dive and body shape do not change.

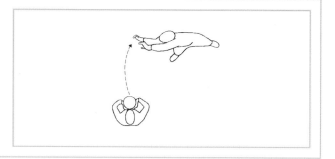

Practice 3

The goalkeeper kneels on the floor in the centre of the goal. The server serves the ball along the ground to the goalkeeper's left, then right. The coach is looking for the direction of the dive (across and forward) and body shape (knee, hip and shoulder).

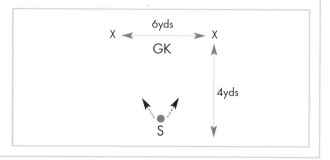

Practice 4

The goalkeeper crouches in the middle of the goal. The server plays a firm sidefoot to the side of the goalkeeper, who falls to the side, getting his hands behind the ball. Repeat on the other side.

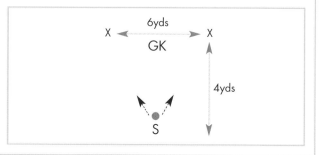

Practice 5

The goalkeeper stands by the post, sideways on to the server, facing away from the goal. On command, the goalkeeper turns and the server throws or sidefoots the ball towards goal.

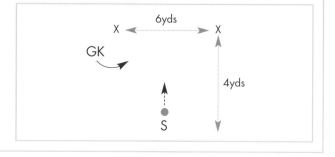

Practice 6

The goalkeeper starts by moving over (one foot or double-footed) or in and out (forwards and backwards) of the cones. The server serves the ball as the goalkeeper clears the second cone. This combines footwork and diving technique.

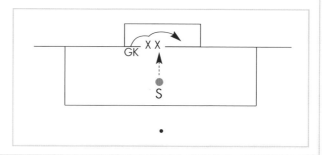

Practice 7

The goalkeeper faces the server but stands behind the marker. The goalkeeper moves his feet forward, then sideways in order to save a ball thrown by the server.

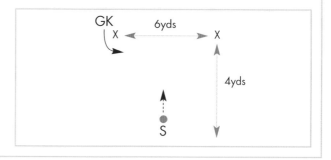

Practice 8

The goalkeeper lies on his side; the server throws the ball a yard to the side of the goalkeeper. The goalkeeper must lift himself off the ground and make his save. The goalkeeper falls down again and the server serves again. This carries on continuously in the same direction for 8–20 reps.

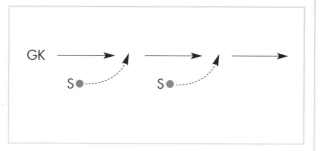

Practice 9

The goalkeepers stand with one ball each on opposite markers. On the coach's command, the goalkeepers try to score past each other with either a throw or volley. The ball must bounce before reaching the other goal.

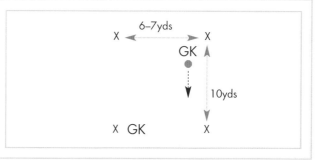

Practice 10

The server serves various shots from the edge of the box – volleys, half-volleys or from the floor and from different angles and heights around the 'D'. This practice brings together narrowing the angle and diving saves.

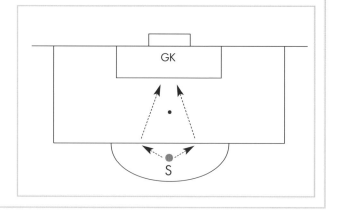

Practice 11

The server serves the ball into the small target, the goalkeeper makes the save and returns the ball to the server, who moves back and throws it into the next target.

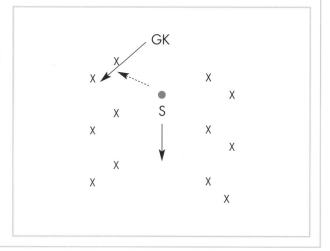

Practice 12

The server on the edge of the box strikes the ball at the goal. As the goalkeeper makes the first save, the server on the six-yard line throws his ball so that the goalkeeper makes a second diving save. Work both the left and right sides from the six-yard line.

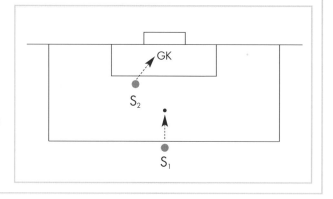

Practice 13

The goalkeeper sits in the middle of the goal, one server on each side; the server plays a firm sidefoot to the side of the goalkeeper, who falls to the side getting his hands behind the ball; repeat on the other side.

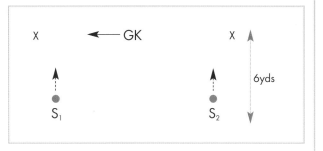

Practice 14

The goalkeeper stands in the middle of the goal, with his heels on the line; the server (six yards out) aims just inside the post with a firm sidefoot; the goalkeeper must react to save.

Practice 15

As above, service is high volley, from six yards.

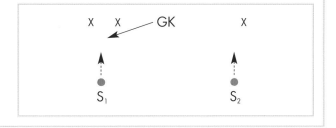

Practice 16

The machine gun – serve the balls alternately, left then right.

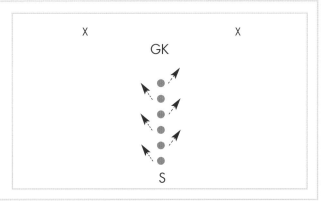

Practice 17

The goalkeeper works around the triangle, while the server serves the ball to the furthest marker – sidefooted, thrown; work to left then to right.

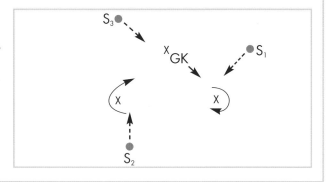

Practice 18

The goalkeeper lies down on his front or back or crouches or kneels; on the coach's command, the goalkeeper gets up and moves to save the shot from the server 18 yards away.

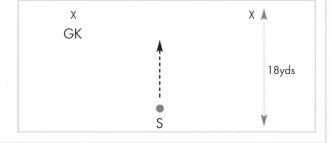

One versus one

Practice 1

The server serves the ball along the ground to the side of the goalkeeper. The goalkeeper slides out on his side practising his technique for diving at a player's feet.

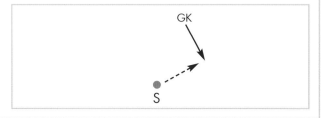

Practice 2

The goalkeeper rolls the ball to the attacker, who controls it and tries to dribble around the goalkeeper. The gaolkeeper should make a save.

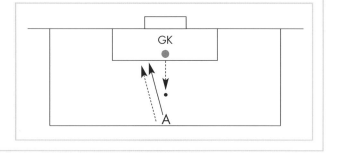

Practice 3

The attacker receives the ball from the server and must take on the goalkeeper who tries to stop him.

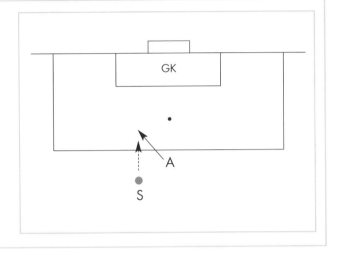

Practice 4

The goalkeeper with the ball has to try and dribble around his opponent. If the opponent intercepts the ball, he then tries to dribble past the first goalkeeper.

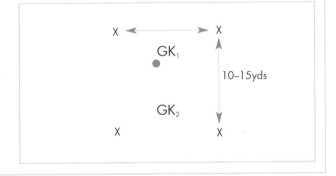

Practice 5

The goalkeeper tries to intercept the ball from the four outfield players who are passing on the outside of the square.

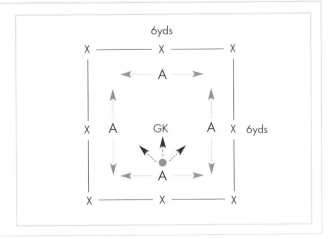

Practice 6

The server plays the ball, giving the attacker the advantage. The goalkeeper must communicate with the defender and stand up, preparing to make the save.

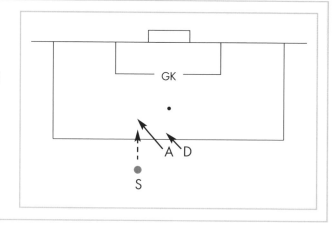

Recovery Saves

Practice 1

The goalkeeper advances to the marker; as the goalkeeper touches the marker, the ball is served over the goalkeeper, who must move his feet and recover backwards.

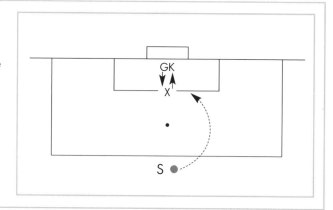

Practice 2

As Practice 1 but the goalkeeper moves up the markers one way and recovers down the other.

NB Service can be by hand or by foot
      if further away.

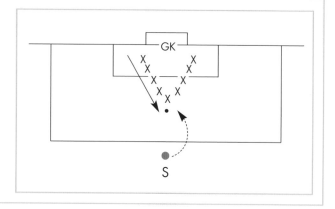

Practice 3

The server volleys the ball at the goalkeeper, who must catch or deflect the ball as A and B are waiting for any dropped balls.

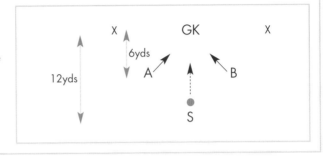

Practice 4

Server 1 shoots at the goalkeeper, who makes a save; server 2 then serves the ball for the goakeeper to make a save, on the left and right side.

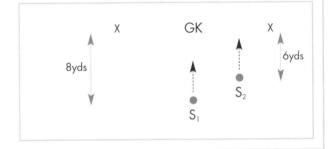

Practice 5

The server serves the ball across the goal; the goalkeeper intercepts the ball; server 1 will then serve the ball for the second save.

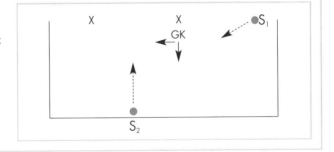

Practice 6

Server 1 serves the ball towards the near post; the goalkeeper goes down and makes a save, then gets up facing play and gets across to the ball thrown by server 2 in the centre of goal; the goalkeeper's view is obscured by those waiting to have their turn.

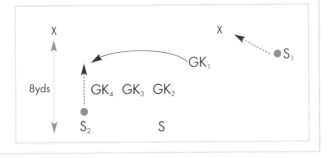

This area of goalkeeping is regarded as being one of the most difficult; goalkeepers who excel at catching crosses are rated highly. Crosses into the penalty area are a major source of goal scoring opportunities in open play; in the 1982 World Cup, 32% of goals came from crosses (Hughes, 1994).[1] This highlights the importance of goalkeepers being able to deal competently with this type of situation. Dealing with these situations requires both sound technique and good decision making. If goalkeepers follow the basic guidelines, these potentially dangerous situations can be managed successfully.

ASSESSING THE FLIGHT AND ATTACKING THE BALL

When assessing the flight of the ball, wait until the ball is kicked before moving. The goalkeeper must assess three things before he moves:

- the line along which the ball is travelling
- the pace at which the ball is travelling
- the trajectory of the ball, including the amount of dip or swerve expected.

Making an early decision to attack the ball or stay and defend the goal is of prime importance to goalkeepers. If the goalkeeper attacks the ball, he must assess its path, call early and not change his mind.

There are three tips the coach should give the goalkeeper:

- move late
- move quickly
- catch the ball at the highest point possible with the arms outstretched.

There are four advantages of the goalkeeper delaying his attack on the ball:

- more time is given to assess the trajectory of the ball
- more time is given for defenders to clear the route to the ball
- late movement means that the goalkeeper must move quickly
- greater height is achieved when jumping for the ball. As greater height is achieved, the ball can in fact be taken earlier than if the goalkeeper moved early, but slowly.

If the goalkeeper makes the decision to stay and defend his goal, he must be prepared to adjust his position, moving into and down the line of the ball, as described in Section Two (page 9).

1   Hughes, C (1994) *FA coaching book of soccer tactics and skills*. BBC publications with Queen Anne Press.

POSITIONING FOR CROSSES

Main coaching points

The goalkeeper's starting position will depend on the:

- position from where the ball is being crossed

- kicking foot of the crosser (if the wide player on the left is right-footed, the ball will angle towards the goal, not away from it as it would if he was left-footed).

Figure 28 shows the position of the goalkeeper in relation to the position of the crosser.

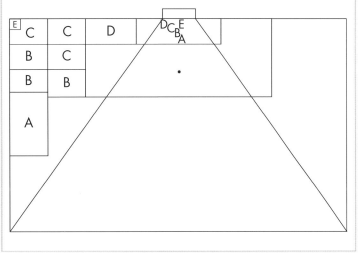

Figure 28

Catching high balls and crosses

When catching crosses, the technique involves jumping and catching the ball in the same way as catching the ball above the head (see Section Two, page 12). Coaching points are provided for each section of the technique.

The open stance

- The goalkeeper keeps his chest facing the ball.

- This enables him to watch a cross from either side and still be able to see any movements made on the opposite side.

- This position also helps him move forwards, backwards and sideways easily (Figure 29).

Figure 29

The take-off

- The take-off should be one-footed to transfer the body's weight in an upward and forward direction.
- The knee of the non take-off leg should be bent to give added lift and protection.
- The goalkeeper should be able to take off with either foot, using the nearer knee for protection.
- The hands should be pushed up through the middle of the body, providing added momentum, making sure the opposition cannot grab the arms easily, and putting the hands and elbows in a better position to catch the ball (Figure 30).

Figure 30

Handling

- The arms should be outstretched in order to take the ball at the greatest possible height and the catch should be made in front of the head.
- The hands should be at the side and behind the ball, fingers should be spread and slightly flexed with the thumbs and forefingers in a W-shape.
- The head should be steady throughout and tilted backwards; the eyes should be kept on the ball (Figure 31).

Figure 31

Catching low crosses

When an attacker has gone to the goal line and the goalkeeper has taken up his position at the near post, the attacker may play the ball back across into play. At this point it is possible for goalkeepers to dive out and intercept the ball. This could either be at waist height or on the ground. This save must only be attempted if the goalkeeper is sure of catching the ball as failure will leave an open goal. It is essential that goalkeepers do not anticipate and commit themselves too early.

dealing with crossed balls

PUNCHING THE BALL

The goalkeeper's priority is to catch the ball whenever possible. However, there are circumstances when the goalkeeper will elect not to catch the ball:

- If there is a strong challenge from one or more opponent, when reaching across defenders and attackers or if there is any doubt in the goalkeeper's mind about catching the ball, he should elect to punch.
- If the goalkeeper is off balance, the ball is too high, beyond the far post or if the goalkeeper is struggling to make a catch going backwards, he may deflect the ball over the crossbar.

Two-fisted punch

This is best used when attacking the ball along the line of flight.

- The fists strike through the bottom half of the ball to propel the ball high.
- The arms end in full extension (Figure 32).

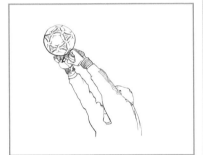

Figure 32

One-fisted punch

This is best used when attacking the ball across its flight path.

- Contact should be made through the bottom half of the ball.
- The arms end in full extension (Figure 33).

Figure 33

Open palm

This technique is used for deflecting the ball over the bar.

- The body should be side-on to the ball and the wrist held firm.
- Contact with the ball is made with the fingers and the top of the palm.
- The head should be steady and the ball watched onto the palm.
- The ball should be propelled in the direction it was heading (Figure 34).

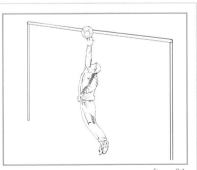

Figure 34

dealing with crossed balls

4

Practices

Practice 1

The goalkeepers rotate after each throw, going around the markers either forwards or backwards depending on their starting position. The service should be a high throw.

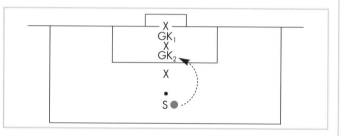

Practice 2

The goalkeeper receives the cross from the server, then distributes to either target.

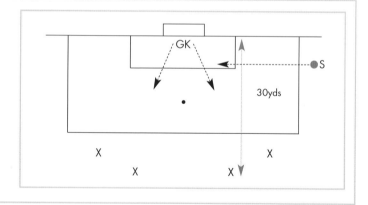

Practice 3

Server 1 crosses for goalkeeper 2 who catches and throws to server 2, while server 2 crosses for goalkeeper 1 who catches and throws to server 1.

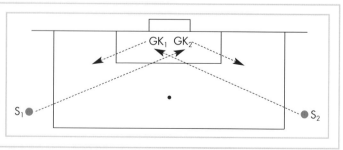

Practice 4

The server throws the ball above the bar, the goalkeeper must jump and push the ball back over the bar to the server (10 reps). The server then throws left and right to get the goalkeeper going sideways and up.

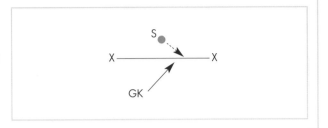

Practice 5

Server 3 serves the ball from the edge of the box, either a half-volley or from the ground. The goalkeeper makes the save and throws the ball to server 1, who controls it and crosses for the goalkeeper who has taken up the correct position. The goalkeeper then catches the cross and throws the ball to server 2 who crosses. The goalkeeper makes the catch and returns the ball to server 3. If the practice breaks down at any time, it starts again from server 3.

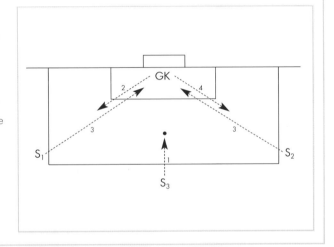

Practice 6

The server calls out a number, then that goalkeeper must come and catch the high serve. The practice progresses by calling more than one number and the goalkeepers come and compete for the ball.

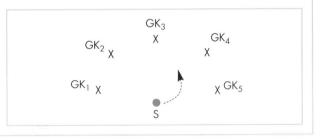

Practice 7

The goalkeeper walks behind the server, who throws the ball up above his head. The goalkeeper jumps and catches the ball above the head of the server.

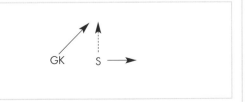

Practice 8

In pairs (1A/2A, 1B/2B), with one in the goal and one on the marker. The goalkeeper on the marker has the ball; he serves his ball high in the air to his partner in the goal, who comes to catch above his head and continues to the marker, with his partner taking his place in the goal. The goalkeepers move to a new marker each time.

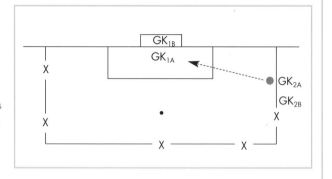

Practice 9

The goalkeeper stands with an open body position. The server serves the ball towards the goalkeeper and the attacker comes to challenge.

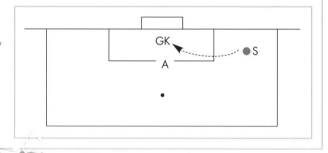

Practice 10

As Practice 9 but this time the service is away from the goalkeeper, towards the challenging attacker.

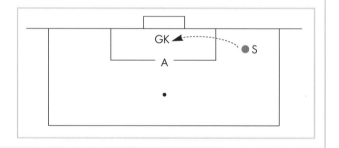

Practice 11

The server throws the ball high for the goalkeeper to come and catch. The goalkeeper starts in a sideways-on stance.

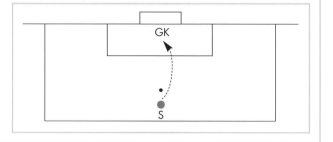

Practice 12

The server vary's service (eg high, low, near and far); the goalkeeper comes and catches the cross. The position of the server changes, therefore the goalkeeper's position also changes.

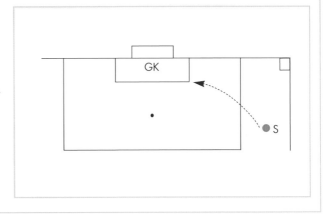

Practice 13

As Practice 12 but service is from both sides.

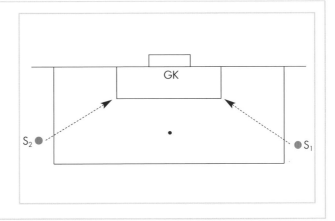

Practice 14

The goalkeeper walks backwards and the server follows, throwing the ball above the goalkeeper's head for him to catch. The goalkeeper is sideways-on to the server.

Practice 15

Server 1 serves the ball for the
goalkeeper to come to catch; the attacker
can only stand still.

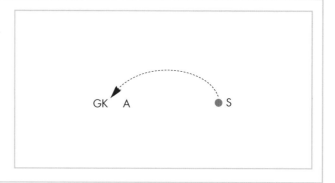

Practice 16

As Practice 15 but the attacker can jump
to try to head the ball. To progress,
add another attacker.

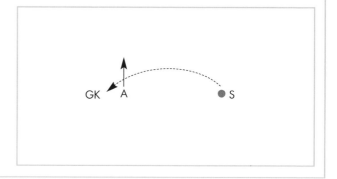

Practice 17

The goalkeeper must position himself for
the cross from the server but also defend
the goal behind him, then open to the
targets.

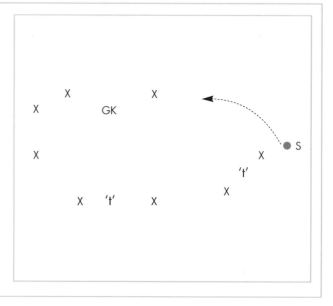

Practice 18

This is a crossing practice with one defender against two attackers; the server plays the ball through the markers for the server to cross A and A attacks the box; D must defend as well as possible.

Coaching Points

- open stance
- quick look into play before cross
- decision: stay or go?
- communication
- action.

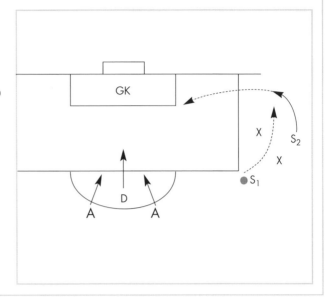

Practice 19

The goalkeeper kicks or throws the ball to server 3 or server 4, who have a touch out of their feet and play the ball wide to server 1 or server 2 who then cross; server 3 or 4 (the player who hasn't played the ball wide) makes a forward run to try to intercept the cross and score (this can be built up into a 'phase' by adding players both attacking and defending).

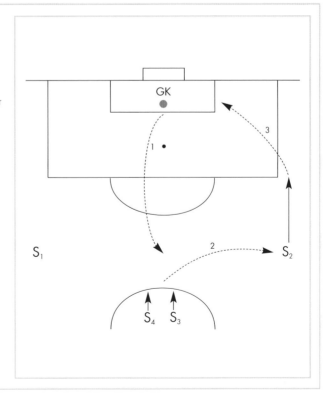

Practice 20

Organisation
The goalkeeper serves the ball to A1 with either a throw or half-volley; A1 controls the ball and plays it to A2 who passes to W1; as W1 receives and travels forward with the ball, A1 and A2 attack the box; W2 can come into the far-post area for an over-hit cross; next time, the goalkeeper serves to A2 so that attack builds up down the other flank.

Progression 1
Add two central defenders and two full-backs – the full-back who is defending on the ball's side lets the winger cross; the other full-back covers round and defends the far post; the central defenders pick up the two attackers as they come forward.

Progression 2
Add two attackers to play against the central defenders – the goalkeeper now serves the ball into two attacking midfield players against one defending midfield player who defends on first touch of the attacking midfield player; the attacking midfield player can play to either winger – full-backs now defend properly.

Progression 3
The attacking midfield players are now free to play anywhere, either into attackers or wingers.

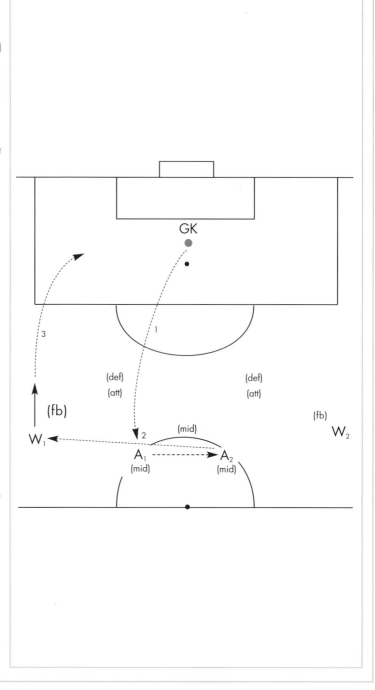

Punching Practices

Practice 1

The goalkeeper lies flat on his stomach, resting on one arm with the other arm in a fist; the server throws the ball and the goalkeeper punches it back to the server's hands (ten punches on each side).

Practice 2

The goalkeeper is behind the goal; the server throws the ball over the bar and the goalkeeper punches it over the server.

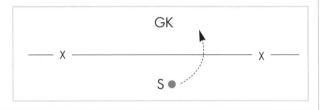

Practice 3

The attacker serves the ball to the goalkeeper, who punches it to B with a two-handed punch:

- kneeling
- squatting
- standing.

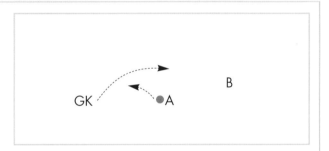

Practice 4

Service as above, but with a one-handed punch.

Practice 5

A serves it to the goalkeeper, who palms it to B:

- kneeling
- squatting
- standing.

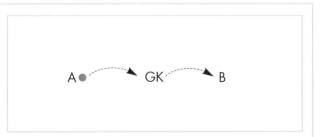

distribution 5

Distribution is a neglected area of goalkeeping, especially with regard to the recent pass-back laws and the six-second law. It is an important skill – there is not a worse situation than a goalkeeper having gained possession, giving the ball away through poor technique or awareness.

At the lowest level, goalkeepers will just get rid of the ball but at the higher levels the goalkeeper will be able to pass the ball. Goalkeepers should be encouraged to pass the ball, especially as they have three advantages over the outfield players:

- They can observe through 180 degrees.
- Once in possession, opponents will not challenge them.
- Passes can be with the hand or foot.

THROWING THE BALL

Throws do not usually travel as far as kicks but the greater speed and accuracy of throwing can make up for the lack of distance and will help the team retain possession. A player receiving a throw must be able to control it early. Coaching points are provided for each throwing technique.

Overarm throw

This is best for covering long distances.

- The body should be in line with the direction of the throw and the weight on the back foot.
- The ball should be brought forward in a bowling action with the arm straight.
- The ball should be released at the top of the overarm swing, as the body weight shifts to the front foot (Figure 35).

Figure 35

Javelin throw

This throw is made quickly with a flat trajectory.

- The arm is bent for this throw; the ball is held beside the head and the body is in line with the direction of the throw.
- The arm is brought forward in a pushing movement with the ball being released at the top (Figure 36).

Figure 36

Underarm throw

- The ball is released from a crouching position, with a smooth underarm swing (Figure 37).

Figure 37

Discus throw

- The ball is held at arm's length and shoulder height, with the weight on the back foot.
- The weight is transferred onto the front foot and the arm brought through at the same time, releasing the ball just in front of the body.
- This is a good technique for propelling the ball a large distance at a low trajectory (Figure 38).

Figure 38

KICKING TECHNIQUES

There are four main techniques – the volley, half-volley, goal kick and running out of the box. Coaching points are provided for each of these techniques.

The volley

- The ball should be held at arm's length and dropped from the hands onto the approaching kicking foot.
- The weight should be transferred forward in the direction of the kick, so that goalkeepers will kick through the ball rather than at it.
- The advantage of this kick is that it will cover a large distance and it is difficult for defenders to get good distance on their clearance.
- The target areas at which the goalkeeper should aim are the channels between the centre-back and the full-back on either side (Figure 39).

Figure 39

The half-volley

- This involves the same technique as the volley but the ball bounces just before it is kicked.
- This technique requires good timing (it is similar to a rugby drop goal).
- The advantage is a lower trajectory, which means greater speed and accuracy (Figure 40).

Figure 40

The goal kick

- The ball is struck with the top, inside edge of the foot.
- Contact is made through the bottom half of the ball, with the non-kicking foot alongside the ball, six to nine inches away.
- The head is steady and looking down at the ball.
- The target areas are the same as for the other techniques (Figure 41).

Figure 41

Running out of the box

- To gain extra yardage, the ball can be dribbled or thrown out of the box before it is kicked. The same technique is used as the goal kick and the ball is aimed down the same channels.
- The ball should be kicked when it is stationary, when an attacking player approaches the goalkeeper.

DEALING WITH THE PASS-BACK

The law change preventing the goalkeeper from handling a kicked pass-back has meant that goalkeepers need to be more skilful with their feet and must be able to deal with both moving and bouncing balls. The key factors to clearing any ball are still the same; the body must be between the ball and the goal whenever possible and the ball must be watched at all times as the goalkeeper attempts to clear.

There are three other key aspects regarding a pass-back:

- Concentration – should be kept at all times
- Angle of support – this is the angle and distance between the goalkeeper and defenders
- Target area – the ball should be played wide to the touch-line.

Making decisions on the pass-back

The goalkeeper has several points to consider when receiving a pass-back:

- Whether to make one or two touches
- The speed of the approaching ball
- The distance between ball, attacker and goalkeeper.

At all times, the goalkeeper must concentrate on the ball – the ball may be on the ground, in the air or bouncing. When goalkeepers have to strike the ball first time because of an opponent's challenge, the aim is to get the ball high and wide, allowing the defenders to re-group.

If goalkeepers use two touches, control is very important. Goalkeepers must get in line with the ball, especially if they are in front of the goal. The control will depend on the nature of the pass-back, its speed and trajectory. The first touch should be in front and slightly to the side of the goalkeeper, then the ball can be driven forwards with a wide, lofted pass. In certain cases, when goalkeepers are not being closed down by an opponent, they will be able to move the ball forward and gain ground before looking for areas to pass into or approaching forwards.

The alternative is for goalkeepers to pass to the full-back. As the goalkeeper is about to receive the ball, the full-back breaks into a wide position and the goalkeeper can then pass to him. In this instance, even if the goalkeeper is being closed down by an attacker, he should be able to clear the ball to the full-back.

General rules

- If the speed and angle allow it, play the ball first time.
- If a touch is needed, control the ball, lift the head and play it quickly.
- Concentrate on the ball.
- Make sure defenders know which is the goalkeeper's preferred kicking foot.
- Get defenders to make moves and create angles to receive the ball from the goalkeeper.

SWEEPER-KEEPER

Many modern teams have adopted a style of play which involves pushing up and squeezing from the back. Therefore the gap between goalkeepers and the last defender has become an even more important attacking space, especially if the defending team's front players are not closing down the attacking team's defenders. Goalkeepers now often have to work as a sweeper would.

The goalkeeper and the rear-most defender must keep adjusting the angle and distance between them, in order to keep the attacking space small. This makes it extremely difficult for opponents to send a ball or player into the space before the goalkeeper or rear-most defender can get there.

The new style of play is forcing goalkeepers to keep their position in or just outside the penalty area for longer. Goalkeepers then have several points to consider:

- The goalkeeper must make an early assessment of the speed of the ball and also the relative distance of defenders and attackers.
- If the ball is over-hit, the goalkeeper will be able to retreat into his penalty area and collect the ball.

- If the ball is near to the goalkeeper but not coming with enough pace to reach the penalty area before the attacker will get to the ball, the goalkeeper must take positive action and clear the ball as far as possible.

- If the ball is closer to the defender than the goalkeeper, the goalkeeper must retreat into the penalty area, positioning himself to receive a pass-back from the defender's head or to receive a pass-back from the defender's feet; the type of through-ball will determine this.

- If the attacker is more likely to win the ball, the goalkeeper must try to recover enough ground from which to form an angle to make a save. If the goalkeeper is too far away, he is susceptible to the lob; too near and he is leaving both sides of the goal open.

The key elements to this skill are:

- good starting position – maintain concentration and awareness

- positive attitude – take charge of the situation

- communication – let defenders know what is happening

- quick feet – be able to adjust position quickly.

The judgement of the through-ball is probably the most difficult part of goalkeeping because goalkeepers must judge the:

- speed of the ball coming towards the goal

- positions of the attacker and recovering defenders

- speed of the oncoming players in relation to the ball and their own position in goal.

is like travelling in a car and trying to guess the speed of oncoming vehicles. A car driver who pulls out to pass a vehicle in front of him, with another coming towards him, must get it right first time or there will be big trouble. This is a similar judgement to sweeper-keepers but thankfully the consequences are not as harsh – the worst case is letting in a goal. No goalkeeper will ever want to concede goals, so frequent through-ball practice is essential. This will improve a goalkeeper's accuracy in judging distances and speed in relation to the position of players.

One factor that will greatly help in dealing with through-balls is the starting position of goalkeepers when the ball is played (Figure 42). If play is in the other penalty area, goalkeepers can afford to be on the edge of their own penalty area – preferably with their last defenders pushed upto or near the half-way line (consider the offside rule and how that can help in defending). Thus, if a very long clearance is hit towards the goal, goalkeepers can come out of their penalty area and kick it to safety or they can retreat back towards their own goal in sufficient time to avoid exposure to the chipped shot.

Figure 42 shows how far goalkeepers can move off their goal line in order to improve their handling of a through-ball or a long clearance, still leaving them with enough room to retreat to their own goal line if necessary. Goalkeepers should be moving forwards and backwards as the play ebbs and flows, they should also move sideways in an arc, depending whether the ball is on the right or left. It keeps them involved and alert, and helps their positional play. In addition, they become a fully participating member of the team.

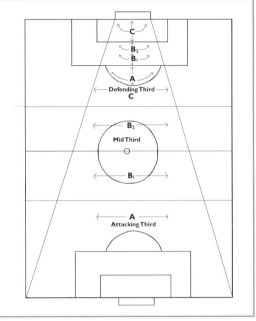

Figure 42

Practices

Key

GK	= Goalkeeper	**X**	= Cone	●	= Ball
S	= Server	**A**	= Attacker	•	= Penalty spot
→	= Movement of Person	---→	= Movement of Ball	◄---►	= Distance

NB When running the practices, always use the coaching points in the preceding section.

Practice 1

The goalkeepers throw the ball to each other using the various throwing techniques. Distance apart varies.

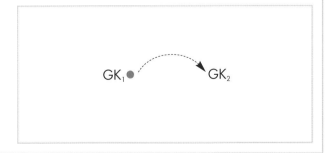

GK_1 ● $\cdots\rightarrow$ GK_2

Practice 2

As practice 1, but using kicking tecniques, accuracy being the key.

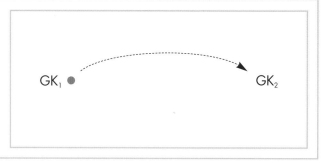

Practice 3

The goalkeeper with the ball must try to knock the ball off the marker with any throw.

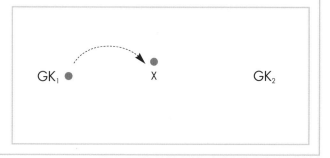

Practice 4

The goalkeepers try to throw the ball through the markers.

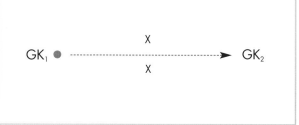

Practice 5

The server rolls the ball to goalkeeper 1, who must try to kick the ball over the server to goalkeeper 2. Progression: the server can follow his pass to put goalkeeper 1 under pressure.

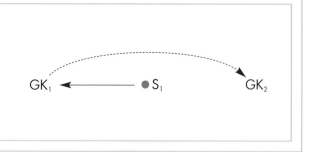

Sweeper-keeper: through balls

Practice 1

The server serves the ball by hand or foot into the marked area. The goalkeeper runs to catch the ball before it bounces in the area. If the ball is served by foot, the goalkeeper may pick the ball up on the first bounce. Progression can be to play the ball along the floor for the goalkeeper to make a smothering-type save.

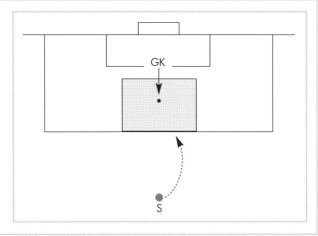

Practice 2

The server plays the ball over the top into the space between the goalkeeper, defender and attacker. The goalkeeper assesses the situation quickly and decides whether it is closer to him, the defender or attacker. He then makes up his mind about whether to go and clear the ball or stay and guard the goal. A progression of this is to move the angle of the through-ball backwards or wider, or add more players until it will build into a phase of play. Make sure that the goalkeeper is in a realistic starting position with regard to the position of the ball and the last defender.

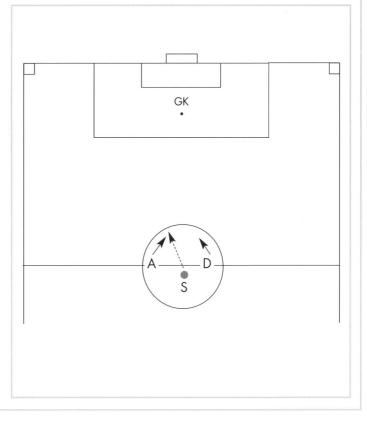

WARM-UPS

1   Run and bounce the ball up and down the gym, using the right hand then the left.

2   Stretch and bend exercises (holding the ball):

    a   hamstrings/calves/back/groin

    b   make a figure of eight with the ball on the floor

    c   make a figure of eight with the ball, changing hands at knee height

    d   lie on back, bend knees and pass ball from hand to hand while moving legs up and down.

3   Two goalkeepers with a ball each, facing each other, a yard to the side of each other, throw the ball straight ahead; they must skip to the side (using the correct footwork) and catch the ball; continue for five minutes.

4   Two goalkeepers with a ball each, facing each other, throw the ball (high and low or side to side) to their partner while side-skipping in the same direction; then skip back in the opposite direction.

BASIC HANDLING

Practice 1

Standing 4–5 yards from the wall, volley or throw the ball against the wall; get in starting position quickly and use the correct handling technique.

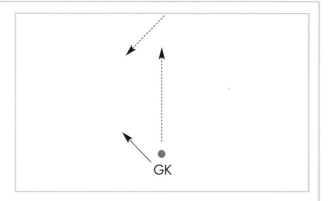

Practice 2

Working in pairs, one goalkeeper sits down with legs out straight; the other stands 3–4 metres away and volleys the ball into the hands of the goalkeeper who is sitting down.

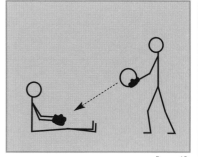

Figure 43

Practice 3

As above, but service is a throw to the side of the goalkeeper; the emphasis is on the goalkeeper getting two hands on the ball and landing on his shoulder – not his elbow – then trapping the ball on the floor, one hand on top, one hand behind.

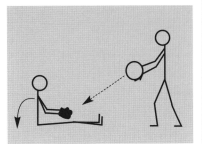

Figure 44

Practice 4

As above, a progression, with the goalkeeper receiving shots from a crouching position (use mats if possible); good practice for collapsing saves, moving nearest leg away quickly to get both hands on the ball.

Figure 45

Practice 5

The goalkeeper faces the rebound wall; server 1 volleys the ball at the rebound wall for the goalkeeper to save; server 2 then performs the same exercise.

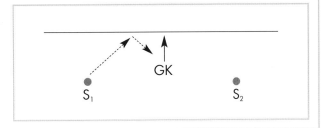

Practice 6

The server throws the ball into goalkeeper 1, who on catching the ball volleys to goalkeeper 2, who then throws the ball into the target man who passes the ball to the server; everyone moves on after five minutes.

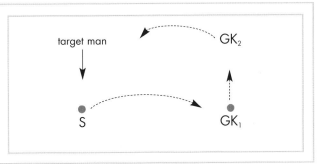

indoor goalkeeping

Practice 7

Two goalkeepers, one in front of the other; the front goalkeeper can either save or leave the ball; if he leaves it, the goalkeeper at the back must react and make a save.

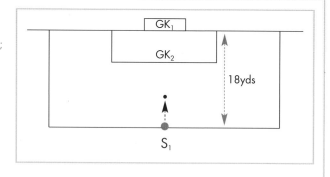

SMALL-SIDED GAMES

1   On a pitch 40 x 30 metres with a goal at each end and 3 metres wide, there is no goalkeeper as such, as the last man acts as the goalkeeper. The players cannot run with the ball – they must pass to each other using the underarm throw technique; the opposition can intercept the ball as it is passed from one player to another; goals are scored by throwing the ball into goal; this game teaches diving saves, movement, distribution and communication (the size of the pitch will change depending on the number of players involved).

2   As above, but passes are above head height; use underarm throw to score – this is excellent practice for catching high balls under pressure, catching on the move and communication (progression: must call before catching and if the ball is dropped, possession goes to the other team).

3   On a pitch 60 x 30 metres with 5 x 30 metre scoring zone at each end; one goakeeper at one end, another at the other end; players must pass the ball to each other by hand for four consecutive passes before volleying into the appropriate scoring zone; change the goalkeeper in the scoring zones at regular intervals.

4   Two v two, 6 metre goal, 10 metres apart – try to score past the other pair with a throw; each team and each goalkeeper has alternate throws.

5   Two goalkeepers, one in front of the other; the front goalkeeper can either save or leave the ball; if he leaves it, the goalkeeper at the back must react and make a save.

REACTION WORK

1   The ball is held by one partner; the goalkeeper stands a metre away, with either hands on head or hands behind back; his partner drops the ball from chest height and the goalkeeper catches the ball before it hits the ground.

2   As above, but one partner has a ball in each hand which he holds out straight (palms up) at waist height; he then allows one ball to roll off; the goalkeeper catches the ball before it hits the ground.

3   Three goalkeepers facing one, two metres away, with two balls between three; one of the three throws his ball to the goalkeeper on his own; he must then find the man who neither has a ball nor has just thrown a ball; continue for 5 minutes.

4   Take two balls and balance one ball on top of the other; then swap the bottom ball with the top ball; repeat.

5   Take two balls and perform two-handed catching with each ball in turn.

Practice 6

The goalkeeper is in goal; server 1 and server 2 try to obscure or deflect the ball past the goalkeeper; if there is a lack of bodies, use large traffic cones.

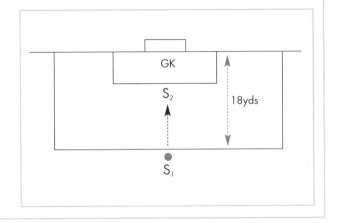

Practice 7

Three, two, one – the server tries to score in all three goals, getting a point for each goal scored; the server can aim for any goal.

Goalkeepers play an important role in the organisation of the team. They are vital to the team-work of a side as they communicate what they can see to help organise defenders. The organisation of defenders is particularly important at set plays, which will be considered later in this section.

COMMUNICATION IN GENERAL PLAY

Communication is an important part of goalkeeping; it should be clear, calm and concise. Goalkeepers have the advantage of seeing the whole of the pitch. This means that they can see situations earlier and more clearly than their team-mates. Goalkeepers who communicate well inspire confidence in team-mates and make the game easier for the team.

There are five main areas where the goalkeeper's communication is vital:

- Blind side situations – the blind side is the opposite side to the ball.
- To push defenders to close or block the ball; the goalkeeper should encourage the appropriate player to close in quickly to stop the shot.
- When defenders are facing their own goal in possession of the ball, unaware of what is behind them, goalkeepers must either support the player and receive the ball or tell the players to kick the ball into touch.
- When the goalkeeper is moving out for the ball and the defender is moving back to play the same ball, communication is vital and must be early.
- To push players up when the ball is cleared, catching attackers offside; this gives numerical advantage in midfield and the team retains its compactness.

DEALING WITH CROSSES

When dealing with crosses, goalkeepers should communicate as early as possible. This enables defenders to:
- clear the ground route for the goalkeeper
- give protection to the goalkeeper
- give cover to the goalkeeper.

Experience is linked to communication – playing experience will help in identifying playing patterns and potential dangers only seen in match play.

ORGANISATION AT SET PLAYS

Set plays are the single most important factor in scoring goals and thus in winning football matches. This sub-section describes the appropriate positions for goalkeepers to stand at the different set plays.

Corner kicks

Goalkeepers should position themselves in the centre of the goal with the chest at 45° to the ball. Their stance should be open, with the foot nearer the goal just in front of the goal line. Communication is again a key factor, not only with regard to the ball, but in making sure attackers are marked.

Free kicks around the penalty area

Figure 46 shows the number of people to position in the wall when free kicks are taken at certain angles. The goalkeeper's position should be on the end of the wall. The keys to success are early organisation, getting a clear sight of the ball and not standing too far to one side of the goal. It is important to stay as central as possible. If the free kick is central, do not have five people in the wall and try to peer around them; have four in the wall as well as a gap and a blocker who is in line with the post. Goalkeepers should position themselves in the gap. If there are too many players in the wall, it can be an advantage to the kicker because the goalkeeper will be unsighted or out of position and the kicker can put the ball where he wants.

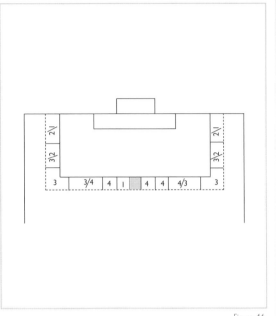

Figure 46

Penalties

In a penalty situation, the goalkeeper must stay on the goal line, only moving sideways between the goal-posts until the ball is kicked.

Most penalties are saved because the goalkeeper moved early. When goalkeepers are facing a penalty, the body position and run-up of the kicker will give the goalkeeper a clue about where the ball is going. At the top level, goalkeepers should know the penalty taker and where they are likely to place the ball. The current trend of penalty takers is either to strike the ball with a lot of power or to wait until the goalkeeper has moved, then shoot. Goalkeepers should try to move up and down the goal line, attempting to distract the penalty taker but be in the centre of the goal when the ball is struck.

The throw-in

When a long throw is taken that may travel into the danger area, the goalkeeper should take up a position in front of the post closer to the thrower. This has two effects:

* It might make the thrower decide to throw it short.
* If it does come into the range of the goalkeeper, he will be able to collect it with his hands.

The main problem from the goalkeeper's point of view is that there is a large number of players in front of him, both attackers and defenders. To catch the ball, the goalkeeper will inevitably have to jump over or around players. In most cases, the safe decision is to let defenders deal with the throw and concentrate on the second ball.

If it is the goalkeeper's team who is taking the throw in, the goalkeeper is not able to pick up the ball directly from the throw but may position himself to receive the ball from a defender via a headed back-pass.

SPECIAL REQUIREMENTS

Goalkeepers are in a specific situation which differs completely from that of the other members of the team. They have the responsibility to correct the faults of their team-mates but have no one to correct their own. Goalkeepers must have a good temperament as they have a limited chance to have a physical outlet for their tensions during the game. In every situation, goalkeepers have to make fast decisions and movements in order to react to the next move of an attacker. The movements required make them more susceptible to injury than other players. Coaches who want to run good training sessions have to be aware of these facts and take them into consideration.

As a rule, the training of goalkeepers has to be functional. They are often trained in isolation from the rest of the team. The only other players involved will be those necessary for the practice, such as wingers and strikers.

An ideal situation is one where goalkeepers report for training 45–60 minutes before the rest of the team, so that the coach:

• can concentrate more on the goalkeeper's training needs
• can take an individual approach to the goalkeeper
• runs practices specific to the goalkeeper's needs.

When the individual training is over, goalkeepers should be allowed to take part in the day's normal training. That means that the goalkeeper's training normally starts early and continues into the rest of the team's training. By training as outfield players, goalkeepers learn to read the game like outfield players and can then benefit from being able to place themselves in the position of attacking players.

Goalkeepers need attentive leadership and care. The coach should have regular talks with goalkeepers to enable them to analyse themselves and their performance, separate from their team-mates' comments. In the team's general match analysis, the goalkeeper's performance must be mentioned too, otherwise some field players might criticise the coach for favouring the goalkeeper. It should be noted that when goalkeepers confess faults, there is opportunity for improvement. When goalkeepers are at fault for a goal in a match, they need encouragement, not aggressive criticism.

To place a club's goalkeepers in order of merit is essential, so there can be pride, confidence and healthy competition; there has to be both a number one and two goalkeeper. Experience has indicated that regular changes of the goalkeepers, for example after two matches, is not favourable to the team. The defence has to be familiar with one type of goalkeeper or confusion can arise. However, if the first goalkeeper is not playing well, he should be replaced by the second for one or two matches before being brought back; this will have the effect of giving the number two goalkeeper some game experience and hopefully spurring the number one goalkeeper on to better performance. When this is done with young or inexperienced goalkeepers, the coach must be very careful to explain to both goalkeepers why he is doing this, to ensure they do not become demotivated or lose confidence.

Tips for coaching all goalkeepers

Coaches should praise and encourage all goalkeepers whenever it is possible, as much of goalkeeping is about confidence. In order to do this, it is essential that the coach knows the goalkeeper as an individual.

As a coach, organise progressive practices and small-sided games that relate to aspects of goalkeeping in match situations. Coaches should focus on the quality rather than the quantity of the training. Coaches sometimes become preoccupied with fitness, and the technique of the goalkeeper suffers. Constant work on the basic techniques will increase the goalkeeper's reliability and hence his value to the team.

Coaches must have a good knowledge of the techniques and be able to recognise faults. The coaching points a coach delivers should be clear, concise, relevant and backed up with demonstrations whenever possible. A coach must remember that everyone makes mistakes and that the ultimate aim is to improve match performance.

coaching goalkeepers 8

THE YOUNG GOALKEEPER

Although the job of coaching young goalkeepers may at first appear to be similar to coaching an adult, it is in fact quite different. Younger performers in all sports differ physically and mentally from older performers.

The muscles and bones of young performers develop at different rates. As the muscles are stronger than the bones, there is an increased likelihood of muscle tendons pulling away from the bone. Bones will also be much more susceptible to breaks in young performers. Children cannot therefore be expected to sustain an adult's training programme. A coach should not introduce high intensity training before puberty, nor use exhaustive warm-ups nor exercise children for too long.

In view of these points, coaches will have to adjust their adult programmes to suit a younger player. The main focus should be on learning skills, rather than on physical fitness. A proper warm-up involving gentle exercise, sustained stretching and more vigorous running to finish should take place prior to training. Every session should be followed by a cool-down activity. Children should always be monitored to see if they are distressed; in hot weather they should drink regularly and in the cold they should always be kept warm (training sessions in both conditions should be short). As children are growing, sustaining a high level of training can make them tired, therefore coaches should make sure that players have enough rest in their sessions and rest time between sessions. One of the key principles is always to work within children's limitations.

Compared with adults, children are limited in their ability to take in information, make quick decisions and evaluate their own performance. Children have slower reaction times than adults, so they cannot be expected to move as early to respond to a situation. They are able to make decisions more quickly if they do not have too much to think about, therefore limiting the cues in each activity, and if they are not confused with technical terms. When children go through puberty, coaches often think that early maturers will continue to excel and that females will improve more than males; this is often a mistake, as the coach must not expect anything. Puberty will affect every child differently.

With young goalkeepers, the practices should be limited to one hour. If they are longer, the technique and concentration of the goalkeepers will start to deteriorate. Practices must be suited to the age and ability of the goalkeeper; it is no good asking young children to do exercises they are not capable of doing, as they lose interest and concentration. The quality of service in practices is important; without reasonable service, the quality of work will suffer. As the standard and age of the goalkeepers increases, the service must change to suit their needs, going from throwing the ball to accurate volleying which makes the practice more realistic and is also good practice for distribution.

Always use the four simple guiding principles:

- Explain what they are trying to do clearly and simply.
- Demonstrate and suggest how they might do it.
- Give enough time for practice.
- Be patient and correct errors one at a time.

Fitness

Soccer players need to develop all-round fitness – endurance, flexibility, speed and strength. However, due to the nature of the position, goalkeepers need to concentrate on different components of fitness from outfield players. After gaining a level of general overall fitness, the goalkeeper's training should consist of mostly anaerobic fitness work (ie short bursts of high intensity exercise). These exercises should be interspersed with generous rest periods to allow recovery and let the goalkeepers work to their maximum. The rationale for this type of training arises from match analysis, which has identified the patterns of work undertaken by goalkeepers; their dynamic acts usually come in single bouts followed by periods of inactivity – on occasions, these acts need to be performed close together (ie a save, then a recovery save). However, it is rare, even if a team is under severe pressure, that more than three dynamic acts will come together before a period of inactivity. It could be argued that because of the systems of play used by modern teams, with goalkeepers acting as sweepers and using more of the pitch (ie bringing the ball out of the box), the physical work done by goalkeepers has increased.

WARM-UPS

The warm-up is an essential area of training for both fitness and technique. The aim of a warm-up is to prepare the body and mind to perform at an optimal level. Goalkeepers need a specific warm-up where they get as much contact with the ball as possible.

The aim of the warm-up is to raise the temperature of the muscles, tendons and joints; this optimises their efficiency. The movements used should simulate the movement in a game situation.

Dynamic flexibility routines should only be used when the body is warmed-up. Dynamic flexibility exercises prepare the muscles so that the joints can be used at their full range of movement. Goalkeepers have different movement patterns to outfield players, specifically in the upper body, therefore they should perform a wider range of stretches.

A dynamic warm-up consists of performing a whole range of mobility exercises. The focus should be placed upon whole body movements. All the movements should be fluid and low impact.

In the past, goalkeepers were taught to stretch statically, but this did not prepare them for the explosive movement to follow.

Examples of dynamic flexibility exercises are as follows:

*   running with high knees
*   running with heels flicked to touch the bottom
*   side-skipping
*   backwards running
*   skipping forwards and backwards
*   controlled leg and arm swings
*   lunging
*   lateral trunk and trunk extensions while skipping.

Upon completing a full range of dynamic flexibility exercises, the coach should move onto the more specific movements incorporating the ball (Practice 4, page 69).

Practice 1

The goalkeepers are in two queues facing each other; they jog up the markers, cross over at the top and jog back down.

GK₁ GK₂ GK₃ → X   X   X   X   X

GK₄ GK₅ GK₆ → X   X   X   X   X

Coaching statement

- focus on quality, not quantity
- work at maximum effort for short periods, then rest to near maximum recovery
- match type situations with realistic practice
- reinforce correct technique throughout exercises.

Warm-up exercises

The aim of the warm-up is to get a feel of the ball and perform some simple stretching exercises.

Running without the ball

1   Jog across the 18-yard box, performing the following exercises:
- knees up
- heels up
- side skipping
- backwards running
- skipping forwards
- skipping backwards
- three-quarter sprinting.

2   Perform stretches, working from top to bottom or vice versa.

3   Jog in single file around the lines of the 18-yard box, performing the same exercises (as per 1) while jogging and increase speed.

Group warm-ups

Practice 1

The goalkeeper with the ball throws, volleys, half-volleys or drives the ball to the goalkeeper opposite in the 3-metre wide goal, then follows his serve. The receiving goalkeeper makes his catch and distributes the ball to the goalkeeper opposite, then follows his serve, and so on.

X   X

GK_1 GK_2 GK_3 ●------▶ GK_4 GK_5

      ▶

X   X

Practice 2

Goalkeeper 1 volleys, half-volleys, drives or throws the ball to Goalkeeper 3 opposite; at the same time, Goalkeeper 2 serves to Goalkeeper 4. Service continues for 10–20 reps, changing the service after each set of reps.

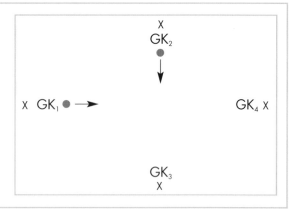

Practice 3

The goalkeepers are one behind the other in a 6-metre goal; the server sidefoots the ball to the goalkeeper who makes his catch and rolls the ball back to the server, moving off to the side after he has done so, so that the server can play the ball to the next goalkeeper coming into the goal first time. Continue until each goalkeeper has made ten catches then change the serve with a volley and a throw above the head.

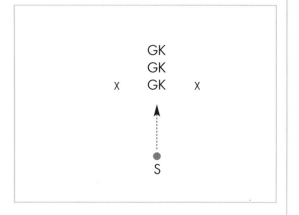

Practice 4

The goalkeepers are in pairs facing each other inside the markers. One of each pair has a ball while the other goalkeeper in the pair side-skips up the markers; they are facing each other whilst rolling the ball to each other. When the first pair reaches the second marker, the next pair can start and so on. On reaching the top, the goalkeepers cross over and jog back down the outside of the markers. Change service: roll, bounce in between, throw at waist height, throw at chest height, throw at head height and throw above the head. Each goalkeeper will work up the markers leading with his left foot then his right.

GK₁ GK₂ GK₃ → X   X   X   X   X

GK₄ GK₅ GK₆ →
      X   X   X   X   X

Exercises with the ball

1 Circle the waist with the ball.

2 With feet shoulder-width apart, pass the ball round the legs in a figure of eight.

3 Make large sweeping circles with the ball held in two hands, reaching to the floor and stretching to the sky.

4 Pass the ball from one hand to the other and with arms shoulder-width apart, stretch down to toes, behind legs, as high as you can, and behind your back while keeping the ball moving from hand to hand.

5 With feet shoulder-width apart, hold the ball between the legs, one hand in front and one hand behind, then release the ball and swap hands before the ball bounces. (Beginners: let the ball bounce, swap and catch.)

6 Sit on the ground with legs apart and roll the ball around the legs and back using the fingertips.

7 Hold the ball in two hands behind the legs, and with legs apart, throw the ball through the legs and catch the ball in two hands in front of the legs. (Beginners: bounce the ball through the legs and catch.)

8 With the ball in one hand, make large circles with the ball forwards, backwards and then at shoulder height with shoulders rolling.

9 Jog forward, bouncing the ball from hand to floor.

10 Jog, rolling the ball in front, then bend and swap to pick up the ball.

11 Throw the ball up into the air above head height, then jump to catch with one-footed take-off.

12 Lie flat on your back, lift bottom off the floor and pass the ball from side to side.

13 Pass the ball below alternate knees in a weave pattern, then increase the speed to a jog.

Paired

1. With one ball between two, stand back to back, keeping feet planted on the floor and twist from the hips as you pass the ball to your partner (approx 10-15 reps, then change direction).

2. With one ball between two, stand back to back, pass the ball to your partner over head, then your partner passes the ball back to you through his legs (10-15 reps, then change).

3. With one ball between two, stand back to back a yard apart (keep feet planted) and twist from the waist in opposite directions.

4. With a ball each, 2-3 metres apart, one throwing high, one throwing low (10-15 reps, then change over). Throw with two hands and catch with two hands.

5. With a ball each, 2-3 metres apart, one throws to left leg, one throws to right (10-15 reps, then change over). Throw with two hands and catch with two hands.

6. With a ball each, 2-3 metres apart, high or low, side to side, but as you catch, take the ball around your waist, then throw to your partner (10-15 reps, then change over).

7. Lie on the ground head to head, one ball between two. You trap the ball between your feet and pass to your partner by bringing his legs up above his head. He then brings his legs up and takes the ball from you by trapping the ball between his feet (3-4 reps).

8. Stand facing your partner, 2-3 metres apart. You have the ball in your hands, while your partner goes backwards. Volley the ball to your partner who catches the ball and throws it back to you. You then move backwards, while he volleys again (10-15 reps). Then change so that you are now working backwards.

9. As 8 above, but this time you serve the ball with your hand above the head of your partner who moves his feet backwards and catches (10-15 reps).

10. As 8 above, but this time you have the ball at your feet and play the ball to the feet of your partner, who stops the ball with his feet and moves backwards quickly. You then play it in again (10-15 reps).

11. As 8 above, but this time you serve the ball by hand or foot a yard to the side of your partner who has to move his feet backwards and sideways to try to get his body behind the ball (10-15 reps).

12. With a ball each, throw the ball to your partner in the air, then he rolls his ball to you along the ground (10 reps, then change over).

13. As 12 above, but with one ball, throw ball to each other on alternating basis, one in the air, one on the floor.

14. In the 18-yard box, with a ball between two, jog around the 18-yard box, throwing or volleying the ball to each other (varying height).

15. In the 18-yard box, with a ball each, jog round with the ball, bouncing, throwing, passing from hand to hand; then on hearing the coach's command, run as fast as you can to the penalty spot/six-yard box. The last player there must perform an exercise.

16. Bouncing exercises - your partner holds the ball at chest height, while you touch the ball with alternate knees; then he holds the ball at chest height, while you flick at the ball with alternate feet, with a bounce in between.

17. Your partner holds the ball below waist height, while you pass your foot over the ball so you are moving your foot left to right across your body, alternately, with a bounce in between.

18 Your partner holds the ball below waist height, while you pass your foot over the ball so you are moving your foot right to left across your body, alternately, with a bounce in between.

19 With one ball between two, first you with ball turn your back on your partner and flick the ball to him through his legs (in American Football snap style), then he catches, turns and snaps the ball back (20 reps).

20 With a ball each, pass the ball under alternate knees, in weave pattern, and increase speed to jogging on the spot.

21 With one ball between two, 3-4 metres apart, stand up with the ball in your hands, while your partner sits down. You bounce the ball in between you and him, and as you sit down while he stands up to catch the ball (10-15 reps).

22 Four goalkeepers in pairs, volleying to each other in cross formation (volleys and half-volleys).

23 Six or more goalkeepers in pairs, with partners volleying and half-volleying across the circle to partners.

24 In a circle, volleying or half-volleying a small skills ball (size 3) across the circle.

25 3-4 metres apart, throw the ball into your partner's body, varying the height and bouncing the occasional ball across.

26 3-4 metres apart, perform accurate volleying (and half-volleying) into partner's hands.

27 8-10 metres apart, perform accurate volleying and half-volleying into your partner (concentrated). Relax after ten accurate strikes and catches.

28 10-12 metres apart, perform accurate volleying into partner (concentrated), then half-volley. Relax after ten accurate strikes and ten clean catches.

29 Small goal (six yards) and in the goal one behind the other. You have the ball in your hands, while your partner stands six to eight yards away. You roll the ball to him and he plays it back, first time to you to make your save, roll it back and move to the back of the queue. Then he comes forward and makes his save (continuing). The service from the server then varies form: into body, above head, easy diving save, stretch and save, serve from hand, bounce before, volley, move further away (repeat).

30 Lying flat on your back, lift bottom off the ground and pass the ball from side to side.

31 With one ball between two, throw the ball to your partner using one hand. He catches the ball using one hand, in the front of line of his body, getting his body in behind (repeat).

32 As 31 above, but with a ball each.

Having the correct equipment is very important to goalkeepers. Unlike outfield players, goalkeepers need more than just boots; they need gloves, specially padded shirts, tracksuit bottoms and a glove bag to keep it all in.

GLOVES

The specialist equipment available to goalkeepers has increased considerably over the past 15 years. Gone are the days of net or cotton goalkeeping gloves for wet weather and bare hands with spit or chewing gum for dry weather.

Goalkeeping gloves have not only become an essential part of the goalkeeper's equipment but they are possibly the most important. They give the goalkeeper an advantage but they are not the whole answer to catching the ball - that is still down to the hands within the gloves. However, they do give increased grip and protection to fingers and wrists. Gloves have changed basic handling techniques. Due to their increased grip, it is now possible to catch the ball securely, at chest height and above, without bringing the ball into the body.

The development of foam rubber for the palms of the gloves has caused a revolution. It encourages younger children to catch the ball as the gloves protect their hands. Gloves come in all sizes, colours and shapes, and range from £3.99 to £59.99, with each manufacturer having its own particular back hand design. At the top level, gloves are supplied for free by manufacturers to goalkeepers. Size is a matter of personal preference; most companies suggest one size too big as this increases the area of foam in the palm, giving more grip. If the glove is too tight, the seams are likely to split when under pressure and if they are too large, the fingers twist when catching the ball. In general, the more expensive the glove, the better the grip. However, the palm of expensive gloves will wear more quickly as the foam is of a softer consistency. It is advisable to wet the palms before playing as this increases the durability of the palm and the grip.

One recent advance is that adidas has designed a unique Fingersave technology, consisting of a resilient, moulded spine on the back of each finger which allows the natural forward curve of the hand but immediately stiffens and resists pressure from the front. This absorbs the energy of the ball in a controlled manner, allowing the keeper to effectively deflect or catch it (Figures 48 and 49).

Figure 47

Figure 48

Figure 49

SHIRTS

With the arrival of the Premier League, goalkeeping kits have become the norm. Goalkeepers now wear completely different kit from the outfield players, as they have been doing in Europe for years. Technology has affected the jersey market; shirts now have foam inserts on the chest and forearms similar to the gloves to aid grip as well as padded elbows and shoulders.

The style of the shirts has recently reverted back to the polo neck of the Bert Trautmann era; it is now more like a sweatshirt design. Traditionally, green has been the colour of the goalkeeper's shirt but now they are often multicoloured as the referees wear green.

With the advent of more foreign goalkeepers to the League, wearing tracksuit trousers has become more popular. The legs are protected from cuts and bruises and kept warm in cold conditions to reduce the likelihood of injury. For training purposes, trousers should be worn as repeated dives may be required and the activity may be intermittent. Trousers will keep the goalkeepers warm and protected.

BOOTS

Technology has affected football boots as well. Modern, lightweight plastics are used in sole construction and specially-treated leathers are used for the uppers to reduce water intake. New technology in upper and sole design has been of benefit to the goalkeeper; adidas Predator and Traxion technology have both benefited the goalkeeper. The Predator, with its rubber fin construction, has enabled the goalkeeper to get more distance when kicking the ball from the hand or the floor. The Traxion has given the goalkeeper increased grip on the turf, especially when moving sideways or when pushing off to dive.

Figure 50

GLOVE BAG

The only other items to mention are those to be kept in the goalkeeper's glove bag, which is a must for any goalkeeper: spare gloves (if possible), a hat for sunny days and possibly a damp sponge to keep the palms of the gloves wet and clean, especially in sandy conditions.

Figure 51

further information

For more information on goalkeeping videos and DVDs and on goalkeeping coaching courses for children and adults, log on to www.simonsmithgoalkeeping.com

sports coach UK runs many valuable courses on coaching. For further information telephone 0113-274 4802 or email coaching@sportscoachuk.org

There is a host of resources available from **Coachwise 1st4sport** which cover all aspects of coaching. For further information telephone 0113-201 5555, email enquiries@1st4sport.com or visit www.1st4sport.com